Who's Tim Sweeney?
(And Why Should You Buy This Book?)

Tim Sweeney is an independent music consultant and founder of the Los Angeles-based artist development company Tim Sweeney & Associates (TSA). As one of the music industry's most highly sought-after experts in the areas of artist development, radio promotion, record distribution, and retail marketing, he has helped dozens of record labels both big (Sony, Geffen, Capitol, Warner Bros.) and small (Calico, Screaming Goddess, King Of Slow) develop the careers of some of their most promising artists, in virtually every musical format.

Now, in this book, Tim Sweeney will teach you what you really need to know about the record business in order to make your release a success. You'll learn: how to make a great-sounding record without spending a lot of money, how to design a winning promotional campaign for your release, how to establish a profitable relationship with a quality distributor, what to say when you're on the phone with music directors and newspaper editors, and most importantly, how to grow the story of your success to build the buzz that will help you sell records and attract the attention of a larger label.

In the past, most of the information in this book was available only to major labels and a handful of independents. Now, for the price of a single concert ticket, you can have your very own private session with one of the music industry's most respected consultants. Read *Tim Sweeney's Guide To Releasing Independent Records*, and take control of your career!

D0645482

Who This Book Is For

If you're an artist and you want to get signed to a major label—this book is for you.

If you're an artist and you want to make a career of releasing records on your own label—this book is for you.

If you're thinking about starting your own indie label and you want to learn how to overcome the obstacles you'll face in getting your records stocked in stores and played on the radio—this book is for you.

If you're an artist manager and you want to learn how to develop the careers of your artists so they can reach the broadest possible audience with their music—this book is for you.

If you're a music writer, or even a music fan, and you want to better understand what it is that artists and record labels have to go through in order to bring you the music you hear—this book is for you.

You don't need to know anything at all about the music business to understand the information in this book.

Tim Sweeney's

Guide To Releasing Independent Records

by Tim Sweeney
& Mark Geller

Tim Sweeney's
Guide To Releasing Independent Records
by Tim Sweeney and Mark Geller
Edited by Mark Geller

TSA Books
21213-B Hawthorne Blvd. #5255
Torrance, CA 90503
Tel: (310) 542-6430
Fax: (310) 542-1300

Attention Colleges And Universities, Corporations, and Professional Organizations: Quantity discounts are available on bulk purchases of this book for educational, training or gift giving purposes. Special books, booklets, or book excerpts can also be created to fit your specific needs. For information, contact the Marketing Department of TSA Books at the address above.

Notice of Liability
The information in this book is distributed on an "As Is" basis, without warranty. While every precaution has been taken in the preparation of this book, neither the authors nor TSA Books shall have any liability to any person or entity with respect to any loss or damage caused or alleged to be caused directly or indirectly by the information contained in this book.

ISBN 0-9651316-0-2

Printed and bound in the U.S.A.

Foreword

The days of being discovered in a bar by a major label talent scout are pretty much over. Sure, every once in a while you'll hear about some new "overnight success", but the majority of bands that are getting signed today are the ones who have marketed and toured their butts off in support of a CD they recorded, manufactured, and promoted on their own. These days, artists like Hootie & The Blowfish, Better Than Ezra, and Lisa Loeb are the rule, not the exception.

Every day, I watch the A&R process at a major label. I can tell you first-hand that the way to get signed is not to send mass mailings of your demo tape. A&R reps want to feel that they've "discovered" the bands they sign. And the way to get "discovered" is to create your own story, create the perception that something exciting is going on with your career.

This book will help you do just that, by providing you with some honest, common sense advice about how to record, manufacture, distribute, and market your own record. By reading this book and releasing your own record, you'll learn a great deal about the inner workings of the record business, and you'll be a lot smarter when it comes time to deal with a larger label.

So use the information in this book to take control of your own career. And we'll be watching out for you!

Steve Ochs
Capitol Records

Table Of Contents

Introduction:

Playing The Lottery

Everyone knows that if you go down to your local gas station and buy a ticket for the Super Lotto, your odds of matching all six numbers are about one-in-a-gazillion. If you buy ten tickets instead of just one, your odds of winning, while still very small, will at least be a little bit bigger. If you buy 500 tickets, your odds of winning will be bigger still, and if you buy 500,000 tickets, you just might win the thing.

And the same is true with music. Let's say you were to sit in your garage and play your music loud enough to annoy your neighbors. There is some chance, however small, that the president of a major label could get a flat tire while driving by your house, get out of his car to fix the tire, hear your music seeping out of the garage, and decide that he had to sign you right there on the spot. It could happen, but the odds are about one-in-a-gazillion.

Similarly, you could make a three song demo tape and send it unsolicited to every major and independent label in the country. Who knows, one of the A&R reps might mistake it for something he actually requested, pop it in his tape deck while he's cruising down Sunset Boulevard and decide he's got to sign you. It could happen, but the odds are about ten-in-a-gazillion.

On the other hand, you could get some money together, record a professional quality CD, release it yourself, get some radio airplay, some press coverage, some gigs, and make a splash in your local music scene. This certainly wouldn't guarantee you a stable career as a recording artist, but it would definitely buy you a few more tickets in that lottery. And it would probably get you a good look from a larger company that might be willing to invest their resources in your career and buy you still more tickets.

My point is this: you're never going to be able to control all the factors necessary to ensure your success as a recording artist (i.e. you'll never be able to buy all the tickets in the lottery)—not even the most powerful major label can do that. But there are a lot of things you *can* do to tip the scales in your favor. Some things, like sending out demo tapes, don't increase your chances very much and aren't worth the effort. But other things, like making and releasing great records, playing great shows, and working hard to build a following will increase your chances significantly, and get you to a position where other people will be motivated to do things that will help you even more.

Chapter 1

What You Want And How To Get It

What Is Success? (Or: You Tell Me)

So you want to succeed in the music business. That's great, but what does it mean? Everyone has his or her own definition of success. For some people, success means getting a cover band together and playing for friends down at the local bar. For others, it means releasing their own records, getting some press coverage in their local music magazine, and maybe doing some touring. And for others (and probably most of you reading this book), it means "getting signed" to a major record label, releasing a string of hit records, and playing to sold-out stadiums around the world.

Obviously, the higher you set your goals, the harder they are to attain, and the less likely it is that you will ever attain them. To make matters worse, the lucky few who do "get signed" and have substantial careers on major labels usually find that the experience is significantly different from what they thought it would be.

My point is not that it's a bad thing to want to get signed by a major label. My point is that if this is your goal, you need to have a clear understanding of what getting signed will *and will not* do for your career. You need to know what you're going to have to do in order to get a good deal, and what you're going to be up against along the way. And you need to prepare yourself for the fact that if you do get signed, you're probably going to discover that it's not the magic cure for all your problems that you secretly hoped it would be.

The road to major label superstardom is paved with a lot of rejections, but it also includes hundreds of little victories—victories that no one can take away from you, even if you never become a superstar: like finishing your first recording, playing it for friends and family and watching their faces fill with pride and amazement, seeing your name in a local music magazine, getting a sincere compliment from a complete stranger, being interviewed for the first time by your local newspaper, opening for a major label touring act, seeing your record for sale in a local record store, being asked for your autograph, getting your first fan letter, hearing yourself on the radio for the first time (or even the hundredth time), and yes, getting signed.

So, if you want to get signed, that's fine. But try to view it more as a step along the road of your success rather than the destination itself. You'll have a lot more fun if you do, and you'll probably end up being more "successful" too.

How Not To Get Signed

Okay. So you're gonna have hundreds of little victories along the way, you're gonna get to see Gramma's eyes fill with pride while she listens to your first recording, and all the rest. That's great, but you still want to know how to get signed. Well, we'll get to that soon enough. But before we do, I'm going to tell you how you're not going to get signed, and that's by sending an unsolicited demo tape to a major label.

For those of you who are new to all of this, let's take a step back and explain exactly what a demo tape is, and why it might seem like a good idea to send one to a label.

Let's say you're an artist with a bunch of great songs, but not a lot of money. You want to attract a record label to market and distribute your music. In order to get the attention of said label, you figure you need to give them some idea of what your music sounds like. So you decide to make a cheap but "decent-sounding" cassette recording of your three best songs (a demo tape), and send it out to

A&R representatives (the people at record labels who are responsible for discovering and signing new artists) with the hope that one of them will hear your music and at least be interested enough to give you call.

Sending Unsolicited Demo Tapes Doesn't Work

Sounds pretty reasonable. The only problem is that it doesn't work. It doesn't work because A&R reps don't want to hear what you're band *would* sound like if you had enough money to make a professional recording. They want to hear what your band sounds like when you *do* make a professional recording. And furthermore, they don't want to hear *anything* they didn't request. So if they didn't ask for it, don't send it.

But what about all those stories you might have heard about bands getting signed off their "brilliant" demo tapes? Well, most of those stories are remnants of the '60s and '70s. In those days, professional recording was prohibitively expensive for most bands, so if an A&R rep wanted to get a basic idea of what a band sounded like, he had no choice but to listen to a low quality demo tape. These days, professional recording is a lot less expensive, and it's well within the reach of many bands to create professionally produced, full length CDs. And they're doing just that.

If you want to go on believing that you can get signed by randomly sending tapes in the mail and hoping for the best, that's up to you. But the fact is: the bands you're competing with are building their own careers and attracting the attention of major labels by making and releasing great-sounding, full-length records. If you want to succeed, you'd better do the same.

How To Get Signed

So you're not going to get signed by sending an unsolicited demo tape to an A&R rep at a major label. Then how *are* you going to get signed? To begin with, you need to understand why it is that a major label would want to sign you, or any other artist, in the first place.

Major labels are, first and foremost, corporations. As such, their main reason for existing is to generate profits for their shareholders. Shareholders don't care whether the world is filled with beautiful, meaningful music. They care about making money. Plain and simple.

Because of this, a major label will sign you only if they think they can make a profit by promoting and selling your records. *Not* because they like your music, or because they think the world needs to hear your music, but because they think they can make a profit by selling it.

If this all seems horribly unfair to you, look at this way. When you ask a label to sign you, what you're really doing is asking them to invest a substantial amount of money in your career. (It can cost as much as $250,000 for a major label to record and promote a single debut record.) If you can't prove to a label that you're a worthwhile investment, or at least that you're as worthwhile an investment as the competition, then why *should* they invest in you?

Most Bands Lose Money

As businesses go, the record business is an extremely risky one. Most major labels succeed in recouping their investments (i.e., making their money back) on less than 10% of their bands.

It's precisely because the record business is so risky that most people who work in it are (contrary to what you might think) very conservative, at least when it comes to doing business. A&R reps, for example, are notoriously skittish (some might say gutless) about signing unproven bands. To understand why this is the case, put yourself in their place:

As an A&R rep, it's your job to find new bands for your label to sign, convince your vice president to sign them, and then make sure that the bands you sign return a profit for the label. This final piece is critical. Most people think that A&R reps just sign bands for the label and then never see them again. But these days, most A&R reps are charged with the responsibility of making sure the bands they sign to the label return a profit. And they are judged accordingly.

If you're like most A&R reps, about 90-95% of the bands you sign will lose money. Even if you are amazingly skilled *and lucky*, more than 75% of your bands—three out of every four—are going to lose money. And every single time one of your bands fails to pan out, your boss is going to want to know why they failed, and why exactly it was that *you* signed them in the first place. And if you don't have a good enough answer, even once, you might very well lose your job. Not a very comfortable picture, is it?

(And the whole scenario gets even more grim when you consider that the average A&R rep gets paid less than $40,000 a year in return for working over eighty hours a week, traveling to some of the most God-forsaken places in America, and of course, listening to hundreds of terrible bands a year to find one or two worth signing.)

Make It Easy For Them

In order to get signed to a label, you to have to do two things. First, you have to convince an A&R rep at the label (and probably his boss as well) that the label will make a profit by investing in your career. Second, you have to make it easy for that A&R rep to "sell" your story to other members of the label so that you'll get the attention you need to succeed.

What They're Looking For

What are A&R reps looking for? Basically, they want to see that you're already accomplishing on a small scale what they hope to accomplish on a large one. Furthermore, they want to see that you've established a foundation on which they can build when they release your next record. For example, they want to see that you've:

1. already recorded and released your own records, preferably in full-length CD format;
2. gotten your CDs stocked in major retail stores—the more stores, and the higher the "quality" (i.e., size) of the stores, the better;

3. sold your product, and lots of it, through *verifiable* sales channels. As far as labels are concerned, if you can't verify a
   sale—either through Soundscan reports, purchase orders
   from your distributor, or (at least) invoices from your manufacturer—you didn't sell it.
4. gotten substantial radio airplay, on both commercial and "priority" college stations nationwide. (Priority stations are the
   ones that have the greatest impact on retail sales.)
5. been playing live at least six to eight times per month in your
   home region, or even better, on tour—and (of course) to
   packed houses.
6. gotten lots of press coverage, most of it positive, both in your
   home region, and wherever you've played live.
7. learned how much work it takes to establish a career as a
   recording artist, and that you're willing to work hard to help
   the label make a profit by selling your music.

If I Could Do All That I Wouldn't Need A Record Deal (Or: Exactly)

Right about now I can hear most of you muttering (or maybe
yelling): "Jeez, if I could do all that, I wouldn't need a record deal."
To which I say: exactly. *The best way to get a record deal, or at least,
the way to get the best record deal, is to show the labels that you
don't need one.* And the best way to show the labels you don't need
a record deal is to develop your career yourself by releasing and
promoting records either on your own label, or with the help of a
competent independent label.

Some of you may already be doing this. To you I say: Great!
Keep up the good work, and keep reading—the rest of this book provides information that can help you dramatically improve your sales
and exposure.

But others of you are probably thinking, "That sucks! I want to
be a musician, not a record seller. If I had wanted to spend my time
selling records, I would have gotten a job at Tower! There must be a
way that I can make it big without having to worry about all this
business stuff...."

To those of you who feel this way, all I can say is: I understand. I myself started out as a musician who wanted nothing to do with the "business" side of the music business. But after a few months on the road, I figured out that if you really want to succeed in this business, you have to understand how the business works. And these days, even that's not enough. These days, you have to make the business work for you by releasing your own records and developing your career.

You need to do this not because I said so, or because the people who run major record labels are sadistic ogres who want to torture you by forcing you to release your own records. You need to do this because other bands are doing it, and if you don't, you won't be able to compete—for fans, for press coverage, or for the resources of a larger label. It's obnoxious, it's intimidating... I know. But it's reality, and one way or another, you have to deal with it.

You Just Might Like It

The good news in all of this is that you just might enjoy taking control of your own destiny and releasing your own records. (And if you do it well, you might even make some money while you're at it.)

Granted, selling records is not the same as making them, but that doesn't mean it can't be fun and rewarding in its own right. And releasing records on your own label will give you more freedom to pursue your artistic vision than you would ever be allowed on a major label, or even a large independent. When you release your own records, you're the boss. You're the one who decides what to record, when to release it, how many copies to press, where to promote, how much to spend, how to much to charge—everything.

In short, running an independent label is not for the faint of heart. It's a ton of work, and it takes constant infusions of enthusiasm and cash. But if you really want to succeed as a performer in this business, it's something you probably have to do. So you might as well throw yourself into it and enjoy it.

Chapter 2

How Major Labels Work

In the rest of this book, we're going to spend a lot of time talking about how to set up your own record company and promote your own records. But before we get to that, I thought it would be a good idea to take some time to explain how major labels release and promote records. For one thing, at this stage in your career, the major labels are your competitors, and it's always good to know what your competitors are up to. For another, seeing how major labels release records just might convince you once and for all that getting signed to a major label isn't necessarily the best thing that can happen to your career. And finally, you can learn a great deal about the obstacles you'll face in releasing your own records by understanding the obstacles the major labels must overcome to get their records played on the radio and stocked in stores. And so, without further ado, I present a brief primer on how major labels work.

Superstars Are The Life-Blood Of Major Labels

As I've mentioned a few times already, the over-riding goal of major record labels is to make money, and lots of it. But, as I've also already explained, major labels, like most record labels, lose money on the vast majority of records they release.

At first that might seem to be a contradiction. How can the major labels turn a profit when only a handful of their artists are able to generate significant sales? The answer is that those few artists that do generate income for the label generate huge amounts of income. And that's no accident.

Everything major labels do is designed to find and develop superstars. For our purposes, you can think of a superstar as any artist that consistently sells at least 3 million records per release. For example, U2, Elton John, Julio Iglesias, Janet Jackson, etc. are all superstars. Superstars are the cash cows that bring in the sales that pay the bills, make up for the losses incurred by developing bands, and keep everyone at the label employed. Any label that fails to maintain a steady stream of stars and superstars will soon find itself in a position of extreme financial distress.

How Do You Make A Superstar?

Creating superstars is not an easy business. For one thing, only a small percentage of records have the potential to be hits, and an even smaller percentage of artists have the potential to be superstars. To make matters much worse, the only way you can tell if a particular record is going to be a hit is to *actually release the record!*

As a result, major labels have developed what is essentially a two step process for creating superstars. Step one is to release as many records as they can given their resources, and step two is to focus their remaining resources on those records show the most promise, and move the artists that created those records up the ladder of success until they achieve multi-platinum sales and "superstar" status.

So there you have a very broad outline of how major labels create superstars. Now let's take a look at the process in a little more detail.

Before The Release

As you might imagine, the process of "artist development" begins in the studio. New bands typically receive between $75,000 and $100,000 to record their first record, and usually work with one of the label's top staff producers or an independent producer.

(Technically speaking, very few bands these days are given any "real" money. Instead, they are given credit in an account that is managed by the label. This kind of arrangement is known as a "fund" deal.)

When the band has completed the recording (called a "studio demo" at this stage), it is copied onto a DAT tape and distributed to various members of the A&R, promotional, and retail marketing staff at the label. The A&R reps then discuss the record and decide whether it is suitable for release. If they decide that changes need to be made or that new songs need to be recorded, they send the band back into the studio to make the necessary changes. This process may be repeated several times until the band comes up with a finished product that the label deems suitable for release (i.e., worthy of the six-figure investment they are about to make in it).

At this point, the record is delivered to the Vice President of Marketing, who theoretically sits down with the promotional and retail marketing staff and designs a customized campaign to market the record. Unfortunately for today's artists, customized campaign design is becoming something of a lost art, and most labels these days tend to use "generic" or standardized marketing plans instead. The benefit of using this type of one-size-fits-all plan is that it allows the label to "streamline" their organization (i.e., reduce their expenses). The problem is that these generic plans fail to provide the individualized care that many artists/records need in order to be successful in the marketplace. (As we'll see later on, one of the biggest advantages of releasing your own records is that you can customize a campaign that makes the most sense for your record, and react to developments during the campaign in a way that would never happen if you were on a major label.)

The Ladder Of Commercial Success

But regardless of whether the marketing plan is customized or generic, its goal remains the same: to develop awareness of the record (and the artist) by getting radio stations to play it, trade publications to chart it, and retail stores to display it. Typically, major label releases begin at the level of college radio and their associated trade publications—*College Music Journal* (*CMJ*)and *Gavin Report*; continue up to the level of smaller commercial stations and their "trades"—*Friday Morning Quarterback* (*FMQB*), *Album Network*, and *Hard Report*; and finally ascend to the level of major commercial stations and their trades—*Billboard*, *Hits*, and *Radio & Records* (*R&R*). In order to understand why releases proceed in this way, you need to understand a little bit about how commercial radio stations and music trade publications work.

The Purpose Of Music Trade Publications

Music trade publications are weekly magazines that contain information that helps radio station music and program directors decide which records to add to their playlists. Each of the eight major "trades" publishes weekly charts of radio and retail sales activity for records in each musical style or "format". Typical formats include: Modern Rock, Country, R&B, Album-Oriented Rock (AOR), Top 40 (CHR) and the newest format—Adult Album Alternative (AAA). For example, the Billboard Modern Rock chart provides information about which records are selling the most units and getting the most airplay at commercial Modern Rock radio stations across the country.

Each format chart is based in part on playlists submitted weekly by various radio stations in that format from across the country. Each station that reports its playlist to a trade chart is called a "reporter" for that chart. The "bigger" the chart, the bigger will be the stations that report to that chart.

Many larger stations report their playlists to multiple charts in multiple trade publications. On some charts, playlist information is weighted so that placing #10 on the playlist of a key station in a major market may result in a better chart position than placing #1 on the playlist of a smaller station in a smaller market. But in general, the way to place high on a format chart is to get as much airplay on as many of the stations that report to that chart as possible.

A Brief Lesson About Commercial Radio

Like major labels, commercial radio stations are corporations that exist in order to make money. They do this by attracting listeners in a particular "demographic"—say, white males between the ages of 25 and 45 with above average income—and then selling advertising airtime to other companies that want to reach these listeners. The higher the ratings (i.e., the more listeners the station attracts) in the desired demographic, the more the station can charge for advertising, and the more money they make.

Music and program directors are paid to keep their station's ratings high. And as much as you might not like it, the way to keep a station's rating high is to play the songs that are known to be hits, and to play them as frequently as possible.

One of the ways music directors determine which songs are the most popular is by consulting the weekly charts published by the various music trade publications. As a result, the best way to get major airplay on commercial radio stations is to work your way up the weekly format charts. And the place to start is college radio.

The Promotion Begins

After the finished master recording has been approved, the label will send it to the factory (which it owns and operates, usually as a subsidiary) for the initial pressing. For a first release, a major label will typically press up about 25,000 CDs at a cost of about $.50 to $.75 each, including printing and assembly. (Yes, that's right—the total cost of production for a major label record is about $.75 per CD.)

The label will then send records to each of the "Level 1" stations that report to the *CMJ* and *Gavin* charts for the given format. At the same time they'll also send records to the "Level 2" stations that report to *FMQB*, *Album Network*, and *Hard Report* (which is named not for the style of music it covers, but rather for its publisher, William Hard). At this point, they may also buy some ads in these trade publications in order to raise awareness of the record with music/program directors and retailers.

About a week before they send the records to radio, promoters from the label will call the stations involved in the release to tell them the record is coming. About a week after the records have been mailed, the promoters will then call back to try to convince the music and program directors at the stations to listen to the record and add it to their playlist.

If enough of the stations that report to *CMJ*'s college chart add the record, it should make it onto the chart. This will get the record some solid exposure among college listeners; and more importantly, it will begin to establish the all-important track record that will convince the "Level 2" stations to play the record, moving the record farther up the ladder of exposure.

Retail Marketing

While the promoters are doing their thing to convince music directors to add the record at radio, it's up to the label's marketing department to convince buyers at record stores to stock the record at retail.

Probably the single most common misconception about the record business is that major retail outlets like Blockbuster, Wherehouse, and Musicland stock every record released by major labels, with little or no prompting from the labels themselves. In fact, nothing could be further from the truth.

If labels can't get retail shelf-space for their records, they can't make sales. And if they can't make sales, they can't make money. As a result, the demand among major labels (and large indepedents) for high quality retail shelf-space is very, *very* high.

Now, if you controlled something that several multi-billion dollar companies absolutely needed in order to conduct their business, would you give it away for free? Probably not. You'd probably do just what the major retail outlets do, which is: charge the labels as much as they can possibly afford to pay.

But wait—taking money from a label in return for stocking and displaying records... that would be payola, wouldn't it?

Retail Advertising

In a word, no. While radio stations are barred by the Federal Communications Commission (FCC) from accepting money or other favors in return for playing particular records, record retailers (which are governed by the Federal Trade Commission) are *perfectly free to accept advertising dollars in return for stocking particular records and displaying them prominently.*

And so they do. Every major record retailer sells packages of advertising that include things like positioning in listening booths, end-cap, and counter displays, and reviews and advertisements in in-store music publications. These packages typically range in cost from $500 for a small display in a few stores to $25,000 for a full-scale national spread.

(Lest you find this idea of "selling shelf-space" to be morally repugnant, I should hasten to point out that most other retail businesses operate in exactly the same way.)

Co-Op Advertising

In addition to in-store positioning, many advertising packages also include a form of promotion known as cooperative or "co-op" advertising. In co-op advertising, the retailer and the record label purchase advertising "cooperatively" (i.e., together) on the radio and TV stations that impact sales in the stores that are stocking the record. This creates additional exposure for the record, which benefits both the label and the retailer. It also sends a message from the label to the radio station that says: "We believe in the potential of this record, and we're going to spend the money necessary to promote it effectively. So start playing this record now, and when it hits, you'll be able to say you were on it first."

Serious Retail Exposure Takes Serious Cash

In short, getting records stocked at retail is a fiercely competitive and expensive business. A major label will often spend as much as $75,000 to create a sufficient retail presence for a single new record.

Assessing Progress

At the end of eight weeks, the label will have spent anywhere from $50,000 - $100,000 just to put a new record in front of a very limited cross-section of the public—namely, college radio fans who live in small to medium-sized markets. At this point, there will be a meeting to evaluate how well the record is doing at radio and retail compared to the other records they are working.

In order for a label to break even on their expenses, they need to sell about 20,000 - 30,000 records in this initial eight week push to college and small commercial radio. But remember, labels are not looking to break even. They're looking for superstars. In real terms, they're looking for records that sell at least 50,000 units in those first eight weeks. They also want to see that the record is getting good response at college radio (charting in *CMJ*) and at smaller commercial stations (charting in two or three of the Level 2 publications: *FMQB*, *Album Network*, etc.)

Records that perform at this level (and/or bands with very powerful managers) get to proceed to Level 3, where the entire cycle is replayed but on a larger and more expensive scale. Once again, the label will send records out to the stations that report to the charts of the relevant trade magazines, which in this case are *Billboard*, *Hits*, and *R&R*. Depending on the situation, the label may bring in independent promoters (i.e., promoters that are not employed by the label full-time) to work the record to the larger commercial stations.

Wherefore Indie Promoters?

Bringing in indie promoters to work records costs the label (and their bands) a lot of extra money—anywhere from $400 to $2,000 per promoter per week. And because promoters typically handle only certain regions of the country, a label might very well have to hire two or more at a time just to work a single record. On a very important release, a label might spend upwards of $5,000 per week on indie promoters alone!

Why is it that a multi-billion dollar international company would spend thousands of dollars per week to hire independent radio pro-

moters, when they already have an entire staff of qualified professional promoters? The reason is that experience has shown that these
indie promoters are capable of getting adds and airplay the label
can't get on their own. And why is this? One word: relationships.

The oldest adage in the music business is that it's not what you
know, but *who* you know that matters. And the people who know
radio program directors are the independent promoters. Most indie
promoters have relationships with stations and their program directors that go back decades. And it's these relationships that allow
them to get records played early and often.

You may be wondering: if labels have to spend so much money
on indie promoters because of their relationships with radio stations,
why don't the labels just develop their own internal crop of promoters who have similar "ins" at radio? The answer is: they do. But
when these promoters have developed their relationships to the point
where they can truly be effective, they often decide to leave the label
and "go into private practice" as an indie promoter, where they can
sell their services to the highest bidder.

Back To The Promotion

So the label brings in the indie promoters, they step up the retail,
co-op, and press advertising, they wine and dine all the influential
radio and press people they can find, and they put the band on tour.

At this point, they'll also (usually) make a video—at a cost of
$25,000 to $75,000—for the song they're pushing hardest to radio.
They'll then promote the video (using indie promoters) to MTV and
a few other music video channels as a way to increase exposure for
the record. Depending on the situation, the label might also explore
other less traditional forms of promotion like advertising on local
cable TV stations or publishing a home page on the worldwide web.

The goal is to move the record up the Billboard and R&R format
charts and sell as many records as possible, preferably at least 5,000-
10,000 per week. At the end of 8-12 weeks, the label will once again
evaluate the performance of the record at radio, video and retail.

If the record has sold more than 100,000 units and charted well, the label might choose to extend the promotion by releasing more singles, making more videos, stepping up tour support, etc. If the record has sold more than 200,000, it will almost certainly get a continued and bigger push. If it has sold less than 100,000 it almost certainly won't, unless the band has a very powerful manager.

So that's pretty much how it works: There are three basic levels of promotion, the first two of which are grouped together. It costs a label about $75,000 to take a record to the first two levels. If it sells at least 50,000 units, they'll invest another $75,000 or so, and take it to level 3. If it sells another 50,000 units, they'll expand the promotion from there. And if they think there's a future for the band, they'll send them back into the studio and do the whole thing over again on a larger scale.

Be A Priority

So that's pretty much how major labels go about breaking new records and artists onto the national scene. Sounds like a pretty good deal: in return for signing away the rights to your next eight records, you get to have a whole crew of talented music industry professionals spending hundreds of thousands of dollars to make you famous.

The fact is, it is a pretty good deal, maybe even a great one—if you can get it. The problem is that only about 5% of the bands (i.e., one out of every twenty) signed to a major label get this kind of attention. These bands are called "priority bands" because the label makes their success a higher priority than other bands signed to the label.

The rest of the bands (i.e., the other 95%) are referred to politely as "non-priority bands". As you'd probably guess, non-priority bands get less money, time, and attention than priority bands.

So what does it mean to be a non-priority band? For starters, it means you'll probably get a maximum of about $10,000 to make your first record. When you're done, your A&R rep may very well decide not to release it, in which case, you will be dropped from the label and be branded as "damaged goods" by the record industry.

You'll probably have a very tough time getting another major label to even consider you, and you'll be forced to go back and develop your career the way you should have in the first place—by releasing independent records.

If, on the other hand, you're "fortunate" enough to have your non-priority record released, your CD will be packaged up in boxes with as many as ten (or more!) other non-priority releases and sent out to a few hundred college radio stations, with little or no consideration given to whether that station is appropriate for the style of music you play.

After one week, a promoter from the label will call up the music directors of the stations to which the boxes were sent and inquire as to the status of the ten records in the box. The music directors will tell the promoter which records they chose to add—usually only one or two at the most. The promoter will dutifully record which stations are playing which records and then tally up the results in a table, listing the records in order of decreasing airplay; i.e., the record getting the most airplay will appear at the top of the list, and the one getting the least will appear at the bottom.

And then, something amazing will happen: the promo/marketing staff will remove the three records at the bottom of the list from the radio promotion and either literally or effectively drop those bands from the label. (Even if these bands aren't technically dropped, they will be placed into virtual exile by the promo staff, and will find it next to impossible to get the label to do anything to advance their careers.) If you're unlucky enough to be a member of one of these bands, congratulations—your career is over.

And if you're not, just wait. Because as unbelievable as it sounds, the label is going to do the same thing with another three or four bands the next week. After only two or three weeks of the campaign, the promo staff will have cut two-thirds of the records from the promotion and dropped seven bands from the label. If you're a musician on a major label, it's enough to make you physically ill—but it's true.

What about the two or three bands that remain? Usually they'll receive very little attention, and will be "dropped" from the label after a few months. If, however, one of them should do exceptionally well at college radio and receive major airplay on key stations, they will usually get more promotional and tour support (i.e., money) from the label. These bands will, in short, become higher priorities by virtue of their proven performance at college radio. With luck, they might even get to make a second record.

The Key Is To Develop Your Own Career

The take-home message from all of this is that getting signed to a major label as a non-priority band is anything but a "big break". In fact, it's much more likely to be the end of your career than the beginning. This is the biggest thing most younger bands fail to understand: *if you don't yet have a fan base, you are much better off trying to build one on your own or with a smaller independent label than you are trying to get signed to a major label.*

Then Why Do They Even Bother?

At this point, you might be wondering why major labels even bother with non-priority bands... if they're not going to invest any resources in these bands, why go through the motions of recording and releasing the records? The main answer is that releasing boxloads of non-priority records is a great way for labels to test out a lot of different bands without spending a lot of money. If the records spark some interest on their own, the bands might warrant some more money and attention. If not, it's no big loss for the label.

Which brings up a very, very important point: record labels, especially big ones, are very often not concerned about the fate of individual bands. Their main concern is that they sell enough records each year to make a tidy profit. They don't particularly care if *you* are one of the bands that are making those records. To put it another way: *It is not safe to assume that your record label will do what's in your best interest.*

An extreme illustration of this point is the fact that labels will sometimes sign bands for no reason other than to keep those bands out of the hands of their competitors. It sounds terrible and cruel because it is. But the fact is that many of the people who run major labels are pathetically childish and petty, and they think nothing of ruining a band's career in order to keep one of their competitors from succeeding. (Have a nice day.)

Chapter 3

What You Need To Succeed

So now we've seen some of the lengths major labels go to in order to break new band, spending as much as $200,000 on a single release just to get it stocked in stores and played on the radio. And even after spending all that money, they only make a profit on about one tenth of the records they release.

If you're a half-way sane person, you might be wondering: "How can I possibly compete in an environment where multi-national corporations are spending hundreds of thousands of dollars on individual records?"

Well, I'm here to tell you that you *can* compete with the major labels. And in the rest of this book, I'm going to show you how.

The Money Thing

But before we talk about how you can compete with the majors, we do need to spend *some* time talking about money. This is, after all, a business you're getting into. And, as with all other businesses, money is the thing that makes it go.

One of the first questions I'm usually asked by new bands is: "How much does it cost to release a record?" The answer is *it costs as much as you're willing to give it.*

Remember: carving out a career in the music business is a lot like playing the lottery. The more "tickets" you can get your hands on, the more likely it is that you'll be successful. To put it another way, the more money you have, the more you're going to be able to do to promote your record and grow your career.

But if what you really want to know is: what's the *minimum* you can spend to make a great record and promote it successfully—my answer is $10,000. This isn't to say that it's impossible to release a record for less than $10,000. But it is to say that my experience at TSA has taught me that in order to make the kind of record and run the kind of promotion that it takes to really make an impact in your market and move your career forward, you're going to need to spend *at least* $10,000, in the following ways:

Recording, mixing, mastering: $3,000
Design, manufacturing, shipping: $2,000
Setting up your record label and home office: $1,000
Promotion (phone, postage, tour support, etc.): $4,000

There's no way around it—ten thousand dollars is a lot of money. Whenever you start talking about an investment of this size, two questions naturally come to mind: 1) What should you do if you don't have the money; and 2) Is the investment worth the risk?

With regard to the first question, my response is: if you don't have the money, figure out a way to get it. If you're in a band of four or more people and you all have jobs, you should be able to scrape together ten thousand dollars over the course of six to nine months. If you don't have jobs, get them.

If you're a solo artist and you don't have ten thousand dollars lying around, you'll need to investigate alternate sources of funding. You might ask your family and friends to see if any of them have the resources and inclination to either invest in your new record company or loan you the money you need to pursue your dream. Approaching friends and family for money can make for a touchy situation, but if you really believe in the potential of your music career, it's an area you can't afford to ignore.

You might also consider the time-honored tradition of starting a new company using credit cards. If you have good credit, you should be able to amass a fair number of low-interest cards on which to draw for your purchases. But beware, some of the companies you'll be dealing with, for example CD manufacturers, may not accept credit card orders.

If neither of these ideas appeal to you, you can find many more suggestions for funding your new company in the "small business" section of your local bookstore.

Which leads us to our second question: is the investment worth the risk? i.e. Can you really succeed at this, and might you not be better off recording a demo tape instead, playing some shows, and trying to attract the attention of a small indie label that would be willing to take the financial risk for you?

Ultimately, this is a question only you can answer for yourself. No one can predict the future, nor can they tell you whether you've got what it takes to succeed in this business.

What I can tell you is this: many of today's major label stars got their start by releasing their own records. It's definitely do-able. And in my opinion, *unless you already have a deal with a major or large indie label, releasing your own record is not only do-able, it's the most effective thing you can do to move your career forward.*

Yes, you could choose to "save your money" and record a demo tape instead. But if you're like most bands, you'll find very quickly that: a) getting signed to even a small label is no piece of cake; and b) you're probably going to have to record at least three four-song demos before you land a deal of any kind.

And even if you do get signed to a label, who's to say that the people who run that label will have the expertise and the resources to really move your career forward? (Most don't.) If you manage to get signed without spending $10,000, but then stagnate on a label that can't or won't promote you effectively, possibly doing irreversible damage to your career in the process, did you succeed? I don't think so.

If you're undecided about whether to release your own record, I suggest you talk to some of the people who run independent labels, both large and small. Ask them what they're looking for in the artists they sign. Ask them what they've done to develop the careers of the artists on their label. Then contact the artists themselves and ask them how they feel about their relationship with the label, and how helpful it's been to their career. Hopefully, this will help you come to a decision you can live with regarding how you should proceed with your career.

But whatever route you choose, I urge you to read the rest of this book. Because most of the things I suggest you do to promote your records are things your label should be doing on your behalf. And no matter what the size of the label you're on, you should always take an active interest in the promotion and distribution of your record and do everything you can to help make your releases as successful as they can be.

Chapter 4

How To Start Your New Label

Still with us after that harrowing discussion of finances? Great. Hopefully that means you've either got the funds you need, or you know where to get them. In any case—no more messin' around. It's time to start your label.

Below is a list of the ten things you need to do to get your new company up and running:

1. Choose a name.
2. Establish an official address.
3. File a fictitious name (DBA) statement with the county.
4. Get a business license from the city.
5. Get a reseller's license from the state board of equalization.
6. Get a manufacturer's ID number from the Uniform Code Council.
7. Design your logo.
8. Print business cards, mailing labels, and stationery.
9. Open a separate bank account for your new label.
10. Set up your new home office.

Pick A Name

The name of your label should be short, sweet, and memorable without being obscene. (For some reason, it's generally viewed as unprofessional to have a label name that can't be repeated in mixed company.) But in any case, you've got to make sure that the name you pick is unique. If you happen to pick a name that's already being used by another label, you might very well find a notice in your mailbox one day threatening you with a lawsuit unless you change it. You are about to spend a great deal of time, energy, and money establishing the "good will" of your name, so it's a good idea to pick one you're going to be able to keep.

Brainstorm with your bandmates and friends to come up with a "short list" of three or four possible names for your label, and then compare them against the listings of labels in the *Recording Industry Sourcebook*, *The Yellow Pages of Rock*, and the listings of "records in print" (e.g. *Schwann's*) at your local record store. Eliminate any names that could "reasonably" be confused with pre-existing names and keep the one you like the best.

Establish Your Official Address

After you've chosen a name, the next step is to establish an official address for your business. I recommend that you establish a business address that is separate from your residential address, for a couple reasons. First, if your business address is separate from your residential address, you won't have to change it every time you move to a new residence. This can save you considerable hassle and expense.

But even if you're not going to be moving any time in the next five years, it's still a good idea to get a separate address for your business. You're going to be sending records all over the country, if not the world. It's a pretty good bet that some of them are going to wind up in the hands of people who might wish to do you harm. And take it from me, you'd rather they didn't know where you live.

To establish a separate address for your business, you've got two options: you can either rent a P.O. box from the U.S. Postal Service or a business mail box from one of the commercial vendors like Mailboxes, Etc. As a rule, P.O. boxes are significantly cheaper. The disadvantage of renting a P.O. box is that most of the commercial shipping companies like FedEx and UPS will not ship to them because there is no one available at the Post Office to sign for the package. If you don't mind having these packages shipped to your home address (and feel comfortable giving your home address out to the folks at record manufacturing plants, distributors, etc.), then you should probably go with the P.O. box. Otherwise, spend the extra money and get a commercial box. (If you're worried that people in the music business won't take you seriously if you have a P.O. box for an address—don't. Some of the most successful indie labels in the country still use P.O. boxes for their addresses.)

File A Fictitious Name (DBA) Statement

Once you've got a name and an address for your new label, you need to file a "fictitious business name statement" (also called a "doing business as" or DBA statement) with the county clerk's office. The DBA is a brief form that announces to the county and everyone in it that you intend to do business under a name that's different from the one your parents gave you. In other words, this statement establishes in legal terms that you and your record label are one and the same. The benefit of the DBA to you is that it allows you to deposit checks that are made out to your record label.

In addition to filing the DBA form, you'll need to publish several regularly appearing notices in a local newspaper recognized to have significant distribution in the county. (The county clerk can provide you with a list of acceptable publications.) You can expect to be deluged with offers from the smaller papers, which usually make most of their income from running DBA announcements. Just pick the cheapest one and get it over with, but be sure to clip out a copy of the announcement the first time it runs, along with the masthead (the title) of the paper, including the date. This will make a great start to your career scrapbook (if you haven't already started one), and will definitely come in handy if you ever need to defend the use of your label name against someone who tries to infringe on it.

Get A Business License (If You Need One)

After you've filed your DBA, you should make a call to the "business permits" division of your local city hall to find out whether you need to apply for a business license and/or a home-business permit. (Some cities don't require you to have a license if your business is home-based.) If you are required to get a license, it should cost somewhere between $25-$100.

Get A Reseller's License

At this point, you should have a legal name, an address, a DBA statement, and a business license. The next thing you need to do is apply for a reseller's license from your State Board of Equalization. For those of you who weren't aware, "equalization" means tax, in this case, sales tax. The reseller's license is the thing that allows you to buy goods as a "reseller" rather than an end-consumer. Translation: with a reseller's license, you won't have to pay sales tax on items like records that you plan to resell to a distributor. Lest this seem like too much of a pain to worry about, I'd like to point out that having a reseller's license is going to save you *thousands* of dollars over the next few years. Get one now. You'll be glad you did.

Register With The Uniform Code Council

For your next bureaucratic trick, you will apply for and receive a manufacturer's ID number from the folks at the Uniform Code Council. This ID number is what you will use to create the bar codes that will allow retail stores to identify you as the manufacturer of your CDs. (We'll cover bar codes in greater depth a little later.) This process will take about three weeks and will cost about $300. I know this is a lot of money, but if you want to get your CDs into major retail stores you've got to have bar codes, and in order to make bar codes, you've got to have a manufacturer's ID number. The phone number is (513) 435-3870.

Designing Your Logo

Now that you've sent off the application for your manufacturer's

ID number, this is a good time to start thinking about designing a logo for your new label. The logo will play an important role in establishing the image of your label (and your band) in the minds of people who have never met or heard of you, so it's important that it look professional. Having no logo is definitely better than having a bad logo, but having a great logo is much better than either one.

The ideal logo will effectively communicate the image you are trying to project, and will reproduce well at a variety of sizes. (Remember, you're going to be placing this logo on business cards, CDs, posters, T-shirts, etc.) To get an idea of what constitutes an effective logo, take a stroll down the aisle of your local record store. Compare the logos used by the major labels like Geffen and Epic to those used by smaller independent labels, and see which ones appeal to you. Brainstorm with your friends about ideas for the logo. Preferably, the logo will have something to do with the name of the label. For example, the logo for Calico Records shows a "calico" cat wearing sunglasses.

If you have any friends who are graphic designers, ask them if they'd be willing to create a logo for you in order to augment their portfolio. (If that doesn't work, offer to make them dinner.) If you don't have any artistic friends, try putting up flyers or talking to people in the graphic design department of your local college. If you still don't have any luck, try calling the advertising department of your local newspaper or music magazine. They might be able to give you the name of an intern who would be willing to do the work for cheap. But remember, above all, the logo must look professional. If you can't come up with something you really like, it's better to just do without, at least for now.

Print Business Cards And Mailing Labels

Once you've got a logo together, it's time to make business cards. Call several local printers to find the best price. (500 is probably a reasonable quantity). You might want to consider printing in two colors rather than just one, but anything more extravagant than that is probably not worth the additional expense. You'll have to provide the printer with "camera-ready" artwork of your logo. In other words, you'll need to give the printer a version of your logo that is suitable to be photographed and printed. Black ink on white paper is usually fine.

NOTE: if you generate your logo on a computer, don't use laser printed output for your camera-ready art—the resolution isn't high enough and you'll get an image that looks unprofessional. Instead, take your computer file to a "service bureau" (ask the printer for a reference if you need one) and have them output the logo in "linotronic" form. Linotronic (or "lino") output has much higher resolution than a laser printer and will give you a much more professional image.

Many bands choose to buy package deals which include stationery and envelopes in addition to business cards. In my opinion, this is probably not necessary. You can create perfectly acceptable stationery fairly easily in Microsoft Word. Custom envelopes are a nice touch, but a lot of the mail you're going to be sending is going to consist of boxes and priority mail. So actually, a better option might be to produce professional looking shipping labels, featuring your logo and return address, and with space at the bottom for the addressee.

Open A Company Bank Account

Technically, the IRS does not require you to maintain a separate bank account in order to take tax deductions for your music-related expenditures. However, for the sake of simplicity and credibility (and to reduce the likelihood of an audit), it's probably a good idea to open one anyway.

Your New Office

Now that you're just about finished jumping through bureaucratic hoops, it's time to set up your new home office. If for some reason, you've already got an office set up in your home—great. (You're *way* ahead of the game.) If not, I'd like to suggest that you decide right now to set aside a portion of your residence for your new business "office". It's best if you can designate one entire room as an office. If not, you should at least try to partition off a section of a room "for business only." In addition to helping you stay organized, creating a business-only area of your home should make you eligible for important tax deductions.

Find Yourself A Good Accountant

And while we're on the subject of taxes, this would be an excellent time for you to find yourself a qualified accountant. I highly recommend that you retain the services of a C.P.A. (certified public accountant), preferably one who has experience working with home businesses. (It's not particularly important that your accountant have experience in the music business *per se*.) If you don't know any good accountants, ask your friends, your parents, your parents' friends, even other small-business owners if they can recommend someone to you. If all else fails, you can probably pick a C.P.A. out of the yellow pages and do just fine.

Your accountant should be able to tell you exactly what you need to do in order to qualify for the business-use-of-home deductions I referred to earlier. These deductions can be worth thousands of dollars each year, so it's very important that you set up your business properly in order to take advantage of them. (Remember: the more money you save on taxes, the more you'll have to invest in your music career.)

Save Your Receipts!

One thing your accountant will instruct you to do is to save all your receipts. This is absolutely critical. You are going to be spending a lot money setting up and running your business, and almost all of it will be tax deductable, from the processing fee on your business license to the money you pay your accountant—but only if you save your receipts. (As far as the Internal Revenue Service is concerned, if you don't have the receipt, you didn't spend the money.) I cannot emphasize this strongly enough. Saving your receipts should not be a habit; it should be a way of life.

The IRS requires that you save your receipts for a period of three years after the end of the year in which the expense is claimed. Some states, like California, require that you save them for four years or even longer. Check with your accountant to find out how long you're going to need to save your receipts.

Get Yourself A Filing Cabinet

And to help you save your receipts, I strongly recommend that you purchase (or somehow get your hands on) a filing cabinet that you can dedicate exclusively to your new record company. Into your new filing cabinet will go the aforementioned receipts, as well as all the other important documents pertaining to your business and your music career: including your business license, DBA certificate, reseller's license, purchase orders for CD manufacturing, invoices to distributors, previous tax returns, contracts, bank statements, phone bills, press kit originals, photographs and other design work, etc. Get the picture? It's a lot of stuff. You need to keep track of it. And a filing cabinet is the best way.

...And A Computer

In addition to a filing cabinet, the other major piece of equipment you're going to need for your home office is a computer. Again, if you've already got one—great. If you don't, it's time to get one. That doesn't necessarily mean you need to spend a lot of money. Virtually any computer sold today will be powerful enough to help you do what you need to do in order to run your business. If you've never owned a computer before, I suggest you buy a Macintosh. (Windows 95 or not, Macs are easier to learn and operate than PCs.) If you have some background with PCs, you might want to go that route, since they're a little bit cheaper and run a greater variety of software.

If you're afraid of computers, or hate computers, and think you can get by without one, think again. Having a computer will save you huge amounts of time and money and make you a more effective businessperson. Growing a successful career in the music business means writing a lot of letters, sending a lot of faxes, tracking a lot of expenses, and maintaining an ever-growing mailing list. Without a computer, you are going to be at a *severe* disadvantage. So be good to yourself—get yourself set up with a decent computer system now, and learn how to use it.

...And A Printer

In order to get the most out of your computer, you're going to need a few accessories. The first is a reasonably good printer. If you can afford a laser printer, that's great; but an inkjet will do just fine. Again, virtually any inkjet printer on the market is going to do just fine for your purposes. Don't spend more than $400.

...And A Fax Machine Or Fax/Modem

Then, you'll need to buy either a standalone fax machine or a computerized fax/modem. (A fax/modem is a device that allows your computer to talk to other computers and to send faxes.) While fax/modems are less expensive, and allow you send "batches" of faxes automatically, standalone machines are easier to set up and use, more reliable, and more versatile.

...And An Extra Phone Line

Regardless of which type of fax machine you pick, you're going to need to get an extra phone line installed in order to run it. In my experience, fax/phone line splitters just aren't practical or professional. You're going to need (at least) two phone lines.

...And A Low-Cost Long Distance Carrier

And while you're getting that second phone line installed, this would be an excellent time to check around for the best long-distance telephone service you can find. Most of the major carriers—MCI, Sprint, etc.—have wholesale rates for businesses. At TSA, we pay less than twelve cents per minute with no minimums or hidden charges. One thing you want to check for when purchasing long-distance service is the minimum increment of billing. You're going to be making a lot of very short calls (leaving messages, sending faxes, etc.). If you go with a service that charges a minimum of one minute for every call, you're going to be paying more than you need to. On our service, times are rounded to the nearest tenth of a minute, with no minimum. So if we make a six second call, we pay for six seconds of service. Long-distance service is a very competitive business, so get several quotes and try to play one company against another for their best rates.

...And Maybe A Scanner

One other piece of hardware that you may or may not want to purchase for your computer, depending on your budget, is a flat-bed scanner. This is a device that allows you to take a "digital pictures" of documents so you can manipulate them on your computer. Scanners are very useful for including photographs and other non-computer-generated art in your press releases, flyers, posters and other documents. A decent one costs about $350. And again, this one is strictly optional.

...And Some Software

Okay, that just about does it for the hardware. Now it's time for the software. For those of you who are totally new to all this computer stuff, software refers to the programs, like Microsoft Word, that allow the computer to do things, like word processing. Because you're going to be using your computer to perform a variety of tasks, you're going to need a variety of software packages, some of which may already be installed on your computer when you buy it, depending on which kind of computer you buy.

A stroll through the software aisles of your local computer retailer will tell you that there a lot of different programs to choose from. I'm going to make some specific suggestions as to what programs you should buy. For those of you who are new to this, I suggest you follow this advice. If you have a little more experience, feel free to substitute as you see fit, as long as you're sure the programs you pick will allow you to get the job done. In either case, you're probably best off buying your software either from a computer superstore or through mail order. They'll have the best prices.

Here are my recommendations. For tracking your business-related expenses and balancing your books: Quicken by Intuit, Inc. The beauty of this program is that is works just like your checkbook, except that it also allows you to assign each expense to an appropriate "category", such as "office-related expenses". This is great because it allows you to see at a glance how much you're spending on various aspects of your business. And when tax time comes around, all you have to do is print out a list of your expenses by category and fax them to your accountant. (We spent a grand total of one hour and $150 doing our taxes last year.) If you buy a Macintosh, Quicken will probably come pre-installed from the factory.

For word processing: Microsoft Word. The indutry standard for creating letters, invitations, and press releases. With just a little expertise, you can also use it to create first rate flyers, invoices, and a just about any other document that consists primarily of words.

For managing mailing lists (databases): My Database, Touchbase, or FileMaker Pro. My Database is inexpensive and easy to use. Touchbase is a little more expensive, but significantly more powerful. FileMaker Pro is more expensive still, but much more flexible (and consequently, more difficult to learn). The fact is, there are a bunch of excellent database programs. You need to find one that fits your budget, while allowing you to update your mailing lists and print mailing labels easily.

If you're going to go the graphics route, and want to produce high quality posters, CD cover art, and other graphics on your computer, then you'll need to buy Adobe PhotoShop and QuarkXPress as well. These programs are expensive (over $500 each) and you can get along just fine without them, so this is definitely an optional expense.

Your Computer Is Your Friend

It's not enough to just buy the computer and the software, you have to learn how to use them. This can be very intimidating, but there are a number of resources at your disposal that can help. First, ask your friends. There's no faster or better way to learn a new program than to be taught by someone who knows what they're doing. If none of your friends know anything about computers, look in computer magazines to see if there are any local users groups in your area. If that fails, maybe you'd benefit from attending a training class or buying some training videos through mail order.

If you don't mind learning on your own, I strongly recommend reading the manuals that come with your software—in particular, the "Getting Started" manuals, which provide examples you can work through for each program. Do these examples several times. If you find the manuals too intimidating, you might try purchasing third-party manuals written by companies that do nothing but teach people how to use software. One line of third-party books many people find helpful are the "Software For Dummies" books. They have titles like "Microsoft Word For Dummies" and you should be able to find them at virtually any computer store.

If all else fails, ask the people who sold you your computer in the first place for help. They should be able to point you in the right direction. But no matter how you do it, you need to learn the basics of using your computer and the software that runs it. Spending a little time now will help you avoid headaches later.

Track Depreciables In A Separate Category

Before we move on to the next section, I want to make one final point about tracking your computer-related expenses. For the purposes of tax accounting, computers and other expensive equipment—including guitars, amps, drums, etc.—are considered to be depreciable items. Unlike smaller items such as business cards and stationery that will be used up in a relatively short period of time, depreciable items are considered by the I.R.S. to have a longer useful life (typically from 3-5 years). Because of this, the I.R.S. will not allow you to deduct the entire expense of your computer or other expensive equipment in a single year, but will require you to deduct a portion of the total expense each year over a span of several years.

This is actually a good thing as far as you're concerned, because it allows you to take a greater deduction in later years, when hopefully you'll be making more money and paying a higher percentage of your income in taxes.

The reason I mention this now is that now is the time you need to set up your depreciables as separate expense categories in Quicken. Consult with your accountant to determine which items are best handled as depreciables. Taking the time now to make sure that your expense categories are set up properly will save you time, hassle, and money later.

Chapter 5

Making Your Record

Now For The Fun Part

Now that you've suffered through all the bureaucracy of setting up your new label and the expense of setting up your home office, it's time for the fun part—creating your first release. Basically, there are two components to any release: 1) the music, and 2) everything else.

I'm not going to go into depth on the subject of how to make a great record. (Hey, you're the artist, right?) But there are a few things I'd like to suggest you keep in mind as you head into the studio.

Single, EP Or LP?

Before you head into the studio, you need to decide what kind of record it is that you're going to release; i.e., are you going to make a single, an EP, or an LP? For those of you who don't know a single or an EP from a hot rock, let me take a moment to explain. A "single" is a record that promotes a single song. Vinyl singles typically contain two songs—one on the front and one on the back. The song on the front is called the "A" side, and is usually the song the record company intends to promote to radio and the press. Vinyl singles usually sell for about $3.

Singles can also be released on cassette (called "cassingles") and CD. A cassingle usually contains two songs, one on each side, and sells for about $3. CD singles, on the other hand, usually contain two or three "bonus" tracks in addition to the featured song. These bonus tracks often consist of modified mixes of the featured song, live versions of past hits, non-album cuts, or covers of songs that were written and made famous by other artists. Because CD singles usually contain more material than vinyl singles and cassingles, they usually cost a little bit more, with a retail price of about $4-6.

"EP" stands for "extended play"... as in, a record that plays longer than a single. As far as retailers (and therefore distributors) are concerned, any record that lasts longer than about ten minutes but less than thirty is an EP. Anything over thirty minutes is considered an LP.

"LP stands for "long play"... as in, longer than an EP. LPs come in all formats. They usually contain about eight to fourteen songs and have playing times of 35-78 minutes. Generally, LPs sell in retail stores for about $12-17.

LPs Are Easier To Promote And Market

What you want to make is an LP, for several reasons. First, because LPs contain more songs, they're significantly easier to promote to radio than singles or EPs. When you send a single to a college radio music director (MD), what you're saying is, "Here's the best song we have to offer... we hope you like it." If he likes it, great. But if he doesn't, you're done. And he's probably not even going to want to listen to an EP or an LP when it's released later because, hey, he's already heard your best song and he didn't like it.

Now imagine that instead of sending that music director a single, you send him a 12-song LP. You ask him to listen to tracks 1, 2, 4, and 6. Now if he doesn't like the first song, he's still got three more to listen through to find one that might work with his audience. And if none of those thrill him, you might be able to suggest yet another track that would work better.

If you listened to nothing but commercial radio all day long, you might get the impression that radio stations get their music one song at a time from the labels. While this is sometimes true at the highest levels of commercial radio, it's rarely true at college radio. College MDs, and even many commercial ones, are much more receptive to playing "alternative tracks" than you might think. By releasing an LP, you're providing them with many more songs to choose from, and increasing the odds that they'll find something they like.

Increasing your chances for airplay is plenty reason enough to release an LP. But there's actually another advantage of releasing an LP that's even more important: you will have a much easier time getting distribution and retail shelf space for an LP than you would for a single or an EP, for one simple reason—LPs sell far more copies than singles and EPs. And because they have a higher retail price, LPs generate more money for everyone involved (including you!) when they do sell.

Remember, a typical vinyl single sells for $3. Of this $3, about $1 goes to the retailer, about $.75 goes to the distributor, and the remaining $1.25 goes to you. After you pay for your cost of production (about $1 per record) and advertising, you'll be very lucky to make any money at all. Now consider an LP CD with a retail price of $14.98. Of this, about $5 goes to the retailer, about $3 goes to the distributor, and the remaining $7 or so goes to you. Subtract out your cost of production (about $1.70 per CD) and advertising and promotion, and you've got a much healthier bottom line.

The retailer and the distributor make about four times as much money each selling an LP as they would a single. You make even more. Add to this the fact that almost no one buys singles and EPs from unknown artists, and you quickly see why retailers won't stock them and you shouldn't make them.

I can hear you thinking: "But isn't vinyl making a comeback?" In a word: no. While vinyl sales have increased substantially in the last five years, sales of vinyl records still account for less than 2% of all music sales, and in 1994, sales of vinyl (as a percentage of the total dollar volume) actually went down. There is no doubt that vinyl continues to be a vital art form, but the fact is, it's just not a significant part of the market. It's unfortunate, but it's reality.

Some of you may find it upsetting that capitalistic concerns like radio promotion and shelf-space should influence the kind of record you make. All I can say in response to this is that I find it upsetting too, but it's unfortunately part of the reality we all must deal with. If you want to succeed as an artist within the retail structure of this country, you're going to have to make some accomodations.

There is an exception to this rule, and that's for those of you in styles of music that do not necessarily rely on radio airplay and retail presence in order to succeed. Those of you in the club/house and rap markets might consider releasing vinyl singles or vinyl/cassette EPs in addition to CDs.

Make It Sound Like It Could Be On The Radio

Most people wouldn't know good songwriting if it came up and bit 'em in the rear end. But everyone—and I mean everyone—can tell if a record "sounds like it could be on the radio". The people at radio certainly can, and so can record buyers, retailers, and distributors. Regardless of the style of music you play, whether it's jazz, country, or punk, you absolutely must make a record that sounds great. Not good. Great.

Find A Great Engineer

So how do you make a great sounding record (preferably without spending $100,000)? First, work with an engineer who has already made great sounding records for other bands. Don't settle for a "student engineer" who will do the work for cheap or free as a way of building up his/her own portfolio, especially if this person is one of your friends. Recording and mixing music is an art form unto itself that takes decades to master, and even then, only a small percentage of professional engineers really have the "ears" and the skill to make your music sound great. All the talk (and all the equipment!) in the world don't make a great recording. Before you agree to work with someone, ask for a demo tape of their best sounding material, preferably in a style that's close to yours. If they can't provide you with a demo that sounds *at least as good* as the recording you want to make, don't work with them.

Attracting a top-notch engineer to work on your project might not be an easy task. It may take you a release or two to build up enough momentum and make enough contacts to become the kind of project that a great engineer will want to work on. That's okay. But you should always try to work with the most talented engineer you can find.

The first thing you should to find a great engineer is to find out what, if any, great sounding records are being made in your area. If you have any friends that have made records you like the sound of, ask them for tips on engineers and studios. If not, try calling the music director or a DJ at your local college radio station and ask them. If you still can't find anyone, try the writers at your local alternative music magazine or newspaper or go down to your local record store and search through the indie racks for records that appeal to you. If you still can't find any promising leads, contact the studios themselves, describe your project to them, and ask them for recommendations.

Try to get demo tapes from at least three engineers who work in your style. Compare the tapes yourself, and play them for your *non*-musician friends to see what they think. (Remember, it's the non-musicians who need to like the way it sounds if you're going to be successful.)

If all the demo tapes have about the same level of sound quality, pick the engineer that you'd feel most comfortable working with. Making records should be fun, and having the right vibe in the studio is a critical part of making a great record. But if one of the demo tapes stands head-and-shoulders above the rest, work with the engineer that made it. Within reason, cost should not be your guiding factor—this is not a good place to try to save a few dollars. If you have to choose between working with a great engineer in a great studio for $55 an hour and working with a mediocre engineer in a mediocre studio for $40 an hour, pay the extra money and get the great sound. I promise, you'll be glad you did.

Do Your Homework Before You Enter The Studio

Step two is pre-production. This is the process of arranging and rehearsing your songs and deciding how you will record them. Whether or not you are working with a producer, you should plan to spend almost as much time pre-producing your record as you do actually recording it. By the time you first step foot in the studio, you should know exactly which songs you plan to record, how they will be arranged, what types of sounds you want to use for each track (including which guitars, amps, and effects you want to use, and how to get access to them), and roughly how much time and money it's going to take to get those sounds. This will save you time and money, and will also result in a better recording, as you won't have to arrange and produce your songs under the pressure of "the clock". As a rule of thumb, you should assume that recording will to take about three times as much money and time as you think it will. (If you think I'm kidding, you've probably never made a good sounding record.)

A Quality Mix-Down Is Critical

Once you've finished tracking, it's time to do the mix-down. Once again, this is no place to save money if it means settling for lower quality. In fact, if you're low on cash and can't afford to pay a great engineer to do the tracking, you should strongly consider working with a less expensive engineer for tracking and then "splurging" on a great engineer for the mix-down. Major labels routinely pay top-notch engineers as much as $10,000 to mix a single track. Obviously, this is way out of the league of any indie artist, but the point is that a great mix is critical if you want to make a great sounding record, so do the best you possibly can.

Here are a few tips to consider while mixing. If at all possible, take a few days off between the end of tracking and the beginning of mixing. This will help you clear your mind and come to the songs with a fresh perspective. And when you come up with a final mix, have the engineer run off some copies for you on tape. Then take these tapes and listen to them on a variety of different sound systems—your car stereo, boombox, home stereo, etc.—and at different volumes. You'll probably be struck by how different the same mix can sound on different systems. That's okay, but you should like what you hear on each system and at different volumes.

Mastering

Once you've gotten a great mix, it's time to send your DAT tape off to the manufacturer to have CDs pressed. Right? Wrong. Before your recording can be turned into a CD, it must first be mastered. Mastering is the process by which a collection of songs is taken from either DAT or magnetic tape and transfered onto Sony 1630 tape (or similar) from which a glass master can be made for stamping CDs. In the process, the songs are "re-equalized" and their relative volumes are equilibrated so that each song sounds as good as it possibly can, and so that all the songs will play at the same volume on the finished CD.

In mixing, the idea is to take a group of individual tracks (vocals, instruments, etc.) and combine them to make a great song. In mastering, you take a group of great songs and combine them to make a great record. Like mixing, mastering is an art form unto itself—one that takes years to "master". And like mixing, mastering is critically important to the success of your project. A bad mastering job will ruin the best music and the best mix; a great mastering job can turn a mediocre recording into something special. So do not—repeat *do not!*— let your record be mastered by an intern at a CD manufacturer. Take your record to someone you know can do the job. And if that means flying it out to L.A., New York, or Nashville, then I suggest you do it.

Assembling The Artwork

Start With The Name

Round about the time you're getting ready to mix your record, you should start to think about how you're going to design and produce the packaging that will contain it. If you haven't already decided on a name for the record, this would be a good time to do so. As a former artist myself, I'm well aware that selecting a name for your record (especially your debut record) is a very personal decision. Having said that, I'd nevertheless like to suggest a few points you should keep in mind regarding the name of your CD.

First, the name should be memorable, without being profane. (Most chain stores are going to reject a record that uses profanity in the title, so picking such a name is just shooting yourself in the foot.)

Second, pick a name for the record that will not be mistaken for the name of your band. This is particularly important if the name of your band contains several words (e.g. Ned's Atomic Dustbin, Deep Blue Something, Emmet Swimming, etc.) If the name of your band sounds like the name of a record, it's probably a good idea to make your first release self-titled.

Most importantly, if possible, you should pick a name for your album that you can tie into the upcoming marketing campaign. This will make the job of promoting and marketing the record much easier. For example, let's say you're trying to decide whether to call your record "Cheese" or "Methodical". In this case, I would suggest you go with the name Cheese because of the obvious promotional tie-ins: for instance, you could include a mousetrap in every package you send to college radio stations, and maybe even mount the CD on the mousetrap with a flyer that reads "Go for the cheese... we dare you." You might even include a mousetrap on the CD cover art, T-shirts, keychains, bumper stickers, and other promotional items.

Another advantage of a name like "Cheese" is that writers can use it to make puns in the headlines of their reviews. I know this sounds ridiculous, but a band name or album name that suggests an irresistible pun has a better chance of getting reviewed. My point is not that you should pick a title for your album based solely on the trinkets and slogans you can devise for it. But you do need to keep in mind that the success of your record is going to depend in large part on your ability to market it. So try to pick a name that's going to be easy and fun to promote.

All About Bar Codes

Once you've got the name picked out, you need to create a UPC code number and a "selection number" for the CD. The UPC code number is the number that will go on your bar code. When you apply for your manufacturer's ID number from the Uniform Code Council, you'll receive a thick packet of information that describes in detail more than you could ever hope to know about bar codes and bar code numbers. To make a long story short... the bar codes used on compact discs contain twelve digits, including the small numbers on the left and right sides. Reading this twelve-digit code number from left to right: the first six digits are the manufacturer's ID number (i.e., the number that identifies which record label released the CD), the next five digits are assigned by the label to distinguish the record in question from their other releases, and the last digit on the right side is a check code, which is used by the code reading machine (i.e., that funky little laser wand or gun they use at the check-out counter of your local record store) to verify that the code was read correctly.

If you look at the CDs in your collection, you'll see that the numbers in the bar code are not spaced according to the 6-5-1 pattern from which they are composed. Why this is I do not know. (No doubt, it's an evil plot devised by the major labels to deter people from starting their own labels...)

To generate a UPC code number for your release, start with your manufacturer's ID number and then add a five digit number that will uniquely identify this release in your accounting records. You can make this five digit number anything you like, with the proviso that it must end in a "2" (this indicates that the product in question is a CD as opposed to a garbage disposal or an air-craft carrier, etc.)

You don't need to worry about the check code digit (i.e., the last of the twelve digits). This number will be automatically generated by the folks who create the film for the bar code itself. (If you really want to generate this number yourself, the formula for doing so is listed in the bar code information packet.)

Once you come up with a UPC code number for your release, you'll need to get a "film" made for the bar code. This film will eventually be integrated into the artwork for the CD when the booklets and tray cards are printed. If you're doing the design for your CD packaging on a computer, you can have the bar code sent to you as a computer file instead.

When you register for your manufacturer's ID number, you'll receive advertisements from dozens of companies that specialize in creating bar code films and files. Pick the one that has the lowest price. Your bar code film/file should cost about $10-$15 plus shipping.

Creating Your Selection Number

After you've created the bar code number, you'll need to create what's known as the "selection number" for your release. This is the number that will identify your CD in the accounting systems of both your distributors and the retailers.

Selection numbers come in all shapes and sizes. For the sake of simplicity, I recommend that you create a selection number that consists of the initials of your record label followed by the five-digit identifier portion of the bar code number. For example, the Calico Records release "When I Was Famous" has the bar code number "781731-00672-0" and the selection number "CR-00672". Got it? Good.

Designing Your Artwork

Congratulations! You now know everything you'll ever need to know about bar codes and selection numbers. (Thank God!) Now for something a little bit more fun—designing your CD booklet and tray card. In case you don't know what a tray card is, it's the little piece of paper that contains the artwork for the back of your CD jewel case. Far be it from me to tell you how to design the artwork for your CD, but (as usual) there are a few key points I hope you'll keep in mind.

Make It Look Great

The finished product absolutely must look professional. Period. If you've never designed a CD cover and/or done page layout on a computer, you're going to need to hire a graphic designer, preferably a very talented and experienced one. If you have a friend who is a designer and who will do the work for cheap, that's great—but only if the finished product looks like something you'd find on the shelf at a major retail record store.

If you're hiring a professional designer, try to find one who has already designed at least several CDs from start to finish. Designing and producing a CD is not a trivial job; there are a lot of details to account for, and if you don't account for them, the results can be expensive at best and disastrous at worst. You'll save yourself a lot of headaches by working with someone who has been through the process a few times already. So spend the money if you have to, but get someone good.

How to find a good designer? Well, you might start by asking your musician friends if they can recommend one. If they can't, try calling an independent record label in your area (if there are any) and ask them for a reference. If that doesn't work, take a trip down to the indie section of your local record store and look for designs that catch your eye. (This can also be an excellent source of design ideas.) If you still can't find anyone, try calling up some of the larger regional or national indie labels and asking them for a reference. Some of the bigger indie labels maintain their own art departments, and some of them will do very hip work for not very much money.

Things To Keep In Mind

As far as the artwork itself goes, make sure that the names of both your band and your record are displayed prominently and legibly on the front cover of the record. Remember, the easier it is for people to identify your record, the easier it is for them to buy it. So do yourself a favor and print your name in nice big letters.

Both spines of the CD (i.e., the sides) must include the name of the band, the record, and the record label, as well as the selection number.

The back of the record must contain the bar code, printed black on white, with suffcient white space around the edges that it can be read cleanly. It's also a good idea to print the name and address of the record label here. Whether to print a list of the songs is a matter of personal preference. From a business standpoint, it's probably a good idea to print the song titles if: a) they're catchy; or b) you have a lot of them.

As for the artwork itself… In general, it's a very dangerous (and usually ill-advised) move to use a photograph of the artist/band on the cover of the CD, except in certain styles like adult contemporary where this seems to be the rule, especially for debut releases. It's sad but it's true: if a music director doesn't like the look of a band on the cover of the CD, he probably won't listen to the record (and the same goes for distributors and retailers). Unless you're drop-dead gorgeous, I suggest you leave the photo on your mother's dresser. If you insist on using a picture, make sure it's a good one, and make sure it's used in a way that's visually striking.

Whatever you decide to use for your artwork, make it visually striking—the kind of thing that would catch a person's eye from ten feet away and compel them to take a closer look. Remember, the cover of your CD is the first thing a potential buyer is going to see of you. So make a good first impression by making a great cover.

I recommend that you limit your CD booklet to four pages. (That's one fold-over card). This will save you money that's probably better spent elsewhere. Rather than print your lyrics on a big fold-out booklet, print a message in your liner notes instructing anyone who wants a copy of the lyrics to send a self-addressed stamped envelope (SASE) to the record company address. In addition to being cost-effective, this is also a great way to find out the names and addresses of the people who really like your music.

Don't bother with things like promotional stickers (the kind that say "Featuring the hit single Big Nothing") or mail-back cards asking for information from your fans. The problem with stickers is that they don't significantly add to the package or increase sales; the problem with mail-back cards is that people just don't return them.

Finally, somewhere in your liner notes you should provide an address (other than your home address) where people can write to send you mail and join your fan club.

Copyrighting Your Material

A copyright is a legal "device" that allows you to prevent other people from using your music without your consent. Technically speaking, there are two kinds of copyrights. The first covers the "form" of the song: i.e., the particular combination of lyrics, melody, and chords that constitute the song itself. This type of copyright is indicated by a small "C" in a circle, followed by the year the copyright was issued or renewed.

The second type of copyright is called a "performance right" and covers the actual collection of sounds that constitute your performance of the song on your record. This type of copyright is represented by a small "P" in a circle, followed by the year the copyright was issued or renewed.

If you're having trouble understanding the difference between the two types of copyrights, think of it this way: the "C" in the circle is what prevents another band from covering your song on their record without paying you royalties; the "P" in the circle is what prevents another label from including *your* performance of the song on a record of their own without paying you royalties.

As far as the lawyers are concerned, you own both types of copyrights on any song you record the moment you record it. However, it's still a good idea to file an official copyright registration form and submit a copy of your record to the Library of Congress in Washington, D.C., in order make a public record of your ownership of the song. If you have an officially registered copyright, you'll have an easier time collecting damages should anyone be foolish enough to use your material without your permission, and you'll also be entitled to recoup your legal fees should you have to take the case to court.

There are several different types of copyright forms. The one you want is called the "SR" form, for "sound recording". You can obtain one by calling the Library of Congress copyright form hotline at (202) 707-9100. You can and should copyright all the songs on your record in a single group for a one-time fee of $20.

Also, you'll need to include both the "C" in the circle and the "P" in the circle, followed by the year the record was created and the name of your record label, on the CD itself as well as the tray card and inside the booklet. It's also a good idea to include somewhere in your artwork a standard boilerplate warning against unauthorized reproduction of your music. My personal favorite is: "All rights reserved. Unauthorized duplication is a violation of applicable laws."

Setting Up Your Publishing Company? Don't Bother

A lot of books about the music business spend a lot of time talking about the importance of publishing. For those of you who haven't read those books, "publishing" refers to the act of generating additional income by licensing the rights to use or re-record your songs for such things as radio airplay, movie soundtracks, foreign language versions, etc.

The problem is that while publishing is unquestionably a significant source of income for people like Janet Jackson, it's usually just a distraction for an indie artist in the process of releasing a first or second record. So, while other books may tell you that you need to form your own publishing company and get registered with a performance royalty collection agency like ASCAP or BMI, I'm going to tell you: don't worry about it, it's just not worth the effort at this stage. If and when you decide to sign with a larger label, you'll have plenty of time to set up your own publishing company and get registered.

Of course, if you happen to know someone at ASCAP or BMI, and they're prepared to help you in your career if you register with their agency now, by all means get yourself registered.

Picking A Release Date

Once you've gotten your music mastered and your artwork together—and before you approach a manufacturer—you need to decide on a launch date for the upcoming release.

The best time to release an independent record to college and community radio is probably early January, just as college music directors are returning to school from Christmas break. If things go well, you're going to be promoting this record for at least the next four to six months, if not longer. By starting the promotion in January, you'll have plenty of time to establish the record locally and then expand to other cities and states before October, when the major labels flood the market with new records in preparation for the Christmas season.

In general, it takes about six to eight weeks to manufacture CDs, starting from the time the manufacturer receives the master tape of the music and all the final artwork. (The manufacturer may well promise you a faster turnaround. That's great, but don't count on it.) Once you have the product in your hands, it takes about eight more weeks to round up distribution and get the pre-release promotion rolling.

Eight weeks plus eight weeks equals sixteen weeks. So, as a rule of thumb, you should approach your manufacturer about four months before your projected release date. If it's August or September now: perfect—you should shoot for a January release. If it's January now, that's okay too. You should be able to get your record out by May, which gives you the entire summer to get it established. Even if it's April now, you can probably get it out by July. But if it's already June or later, don't push it. Save the manufacturing until September and shoot for a January release. (And remember to use next year as the year of copyright so that your record isn't already "a year old" when it comes out.)

How Many CDs Should You Make?

Now that you know what you're going to make and when you're going to make it, you need to decide how many to produce. If you're planning a regional or national release, I suggest you start with somewhere between 2,000 and 2,500 CDs. If that seems like a lot, keep in mind that you're going to be giving away a substantial number of these—typically at least 600—as demo copies. (200 in your radio mail-outs, another 300 as follow-up copies for the stations that add your record, 50 to press outlets, and another 50 to distributor and sales reps and other "mover and shaker" types.) If you're planning a smaller release, you can probably get away with 1,000 or 1,500.

One important thing to keep in mind about pressing CDs is that the limiting step in CD production is not the manufacturing or assembly of the CDs themselves but the printing of the booklets and tray cards. If you think you're going to need additional CDs beyond your initial order, consider printing the additional booklets and tray cards at the time you place the initial order. For example, if your first pressing is for 2,500 CDs, you might print a total of 5,000 booklets and tray cards, which would leave you with 2,500 extra booklets and tray cards for subsequent orders. Many printers and CD production brokers offer substantial price breaks on orders of 4,000 booklets or more. Be sure to ask if yours does. (You may actually wind up paying less for 4,000 booklets than you would for 2,500.)

You Get What You Pay For

Many CD brokers offer "package deals" in which they will not only manufacture your CDs and print your "graphics" (booklets and tray cards), but they will also perform the mastering and design the artwork. As you can probably guess, I'm not a big fan of these deals. I've said it before, but I'm going to say it again: *a great mastering job is absolutely critical to the success of your project*. Most of the "mastering services" provided by CD brokers consist of merely transfering tracks from the DAT mix tape onto a Sony 1630 with no alteration. Please don't let this happen to your music. If you care enough about your music to want to spend your life sharing it with the public, then you should care enough to have it properly mastered.

The same goes with your artwork. The only way to come up with a great design for your package—one that truly captures the spirit of your music—is to develop a relationship with a talented designer in which you can effectively communicate just what it is that you're trying to accomplish in both your music and its marketing. Good design is a process of give-and-take and numerous revisions. If you send your package off to a CD broker and hire them to do the design, it's a pretty good bet that the design you get back will be generic and boring, and therefore worthless. Again: this is your music we're talking about here. Care enough to give it a great presentation.

Aside from that, my only advice in selecting a CD broker is to focus on reliability and price. If any of your friends have pressed CDs, ask them for references. And be sure to ask them what it was like to deal with the people at the broker: were they helpful and responsive? Did they keep their promises? Were there any hidden costs? etc. If none of your friends have pressed CDs, take a trip down to your local record store, etc., and get the names and addresses of some local indie labels and ask them for referrals.

How much should it cost? That depends on what you buy. I recommend that you buy a "package" that includes the manufacturing of the CDs, assembly of the CDs and "graphics" into jewel cases (those are the plastic CD cases that hold CDs), and shrinkwrapping. 2,000 CDs assembled and shrinkwrapped should cost you about $1.30-$1.50 per CD. (Remember, this price does not include the cost of printing the graphics.) The more CDs you make, the lower your price should be.

Don't Pay Extra For Your Glass Master

Watch out for brokers that want to charge you extra for creating the glass master. (Think of the glass master as the "mold" from which your CDs will be replicated. Creating a glass master is *not* the same thing as "mastering" discussed above.) Some brokers will try to charge as much as $300 for creating the glass master, but many will throw it in for free on orders of 2,000 CDs or more. If your broker tries to charge you extra for the glass master, ask them to throw it in for free. If they won't, tell them you're thinking of going to someone else who will. If they *still* won't, then find another broker.

Where To Print Your Graphics

Another thing you'll need to decide before manufacturing is whether to print the "graphics" through the broker or to print them locally and then ship them to the CD plant. The advantage of printing them locally is that you have more control over the quality of the printing job. If the printer is local, you and/or your designer can check the job on the press to make sure the colors are right, etc. This might not sound all that important, but imagine how disappointed you'd be to open up your first delivery of CDs and find that the beautiful red logo you spent two weeks designing came out orange. Also, if there's any problem with the artwork for the job—damaged computer files, missing files, artwork that doesn't fit the size specifications, etc.—it's a lot easier and faster to fix it locally than from 2,000 miles away.

The advantages of printing it through the broker are mainly cost and convenience. Because most brokers do high volume, they usually offer better prices than all-purpose printers. Most brokers offer printing packages that include 4-panel booklets (i.e., a single rectangular page that folds over once onto itself) with full color on the cover and the tray cards for about $0.15-$0.20 each when purchased along with CD pressing, assembly, and shrinkwrapping.

In addition to saving you money in shipping and printing, a good broker can also spot problems with the artwork before it goes to print, saving time, money, and headaches. Given all of that, I recommend that you use a broker as long as your printing job is fairly straightforward. (And I definitely recommend that you try to keep your printing job straightforward!) But if you've already been working with a local printer whom you know and trust, you'd probably do well to continue in that relationship.

Avoid Headaches, Hidden Costs

Before you send the broker any money, *make sure you get a complete written list of any and all possible additional charges*. If you don't, you may be in for a very unpleasant surprise when you get your bill.

If you're going to have the broker do the printing, be sure to discuss how you're going to handle the proofing of the artwork before the printing begins. (Your designer should be able to help you with this.) You'll also need to discuss how the product will be shipped to you after it has been produced and assembled. Remember: you're the one who's going to be paying the freight bill, so make sure the shipping arrangements aren't unnecessarily extravagant.

Plus Or Minus 10%

Unfortunately, it's industry standard that you'll have to pay for the entire job before it goes to press. To make matters worse, you'll probably have to prepay an overage equal to 10% of the job, with the agreement that you'll receive a refund for any CDs not shipped to you. The reason for this is that CD manufacturing is apparently still something of an inexact science, and they can't tell how many of the CDs they produce will be functional until after they've made them.

Agree On A Schedule

The other thing you'll need to discuss with your broker before you send him any money is the production schedule. Set out a date by which you'll send him the master tape and the artwork (or the printed graphics) and establish a realistic date by which you can expect to receive the finished product.

The amount of time it takes the broker to go from master tape to finished product is called the "turn-time", and it can vary dramatically depending on the broker, the time of year, the size of your order, and most importantly your relationship with the broker. If you're on a rigid schedule—as you will be if your promotion is set to begin less than two months after you receive the discs—make sure you inform your broker ahead of time, and ask him for an honest assessment of whether he's going to be able to provide you the with the CDs on time. You'll never be able to get a broker to "guarantee" a delivery date because much of what goes on at the actual manufacturing plant is beyond his control. But if you tell him up-front and honestly what you need from him, you're much more likely to get it.

Have Your Demos Punched

A few more things before we leave this section. First, it's a good idea to have about 500 of your CDs sent to you *without* shrinkwrapping. These are going to be demo copies; they don't need to be shrinkwrapped, so there's no reason to pay for it. (And since shrinkwrapping usually costs about $0.05 per CD, this should save you about $25.)

Also, ask your broker if he can have these same 500 CDs "punched". This means that the manufacturer will literally drill a hole through the bar codes of these CDs, which will make it more difficult for people at radio and the press to sell your demos as used (or even new) CDs to local record stores. Believe it or not, there are people in this world who actually steal demos and sell them for personal gain. Because there's easy money to be made, the temptation to steal demos is great, so keep the honest people honest by punching your demos. A top-notch broker shouldn't charge you extra for this service.

Incidentally, if your manufacturer doesn't have the facilities to punch your demos, you can achieve the desired effect yourself by hand: just open up the CD, pull out the booklet, and clip off the upper right corner about a half-inch over and a half-inch down using a pair of scissors. "But that makes it look so ugly and unprofessional!" you say. Exactly. That's why no one will buy it. But music directors won't hold it against you. I promise.

Taking Delivery

One last thing about manufacturing, and that's taking delivery of your records. After the records have been manufactured and assembled, they will be shipped to you *at your expense*. Verify with your broker how the CDs will be shipped. If they're being sent to you by "freight" (as opposed to UPS, etc.), ask whether they'll be delivered by a semi truck. If so, be sure to verify that the semi will be able to deliver the records to the shipping address you've specified. If you live in a residential suburb, your street may be off-limits to a semi. If this is the case, you'll either need to provide an alternate shipping address (possibly your work address) or instruct the manufacturer to have the freight company drop the records at their warehouse, where you can come pick them up yourself.

If you're already set up with a distributor, you might want to consider "drop-shipping" the records (i.e., having them shipped directly to the distributor, in a previously agreed upon quantity). This will save you the time and expense of shipping the records twice.

Making Your Press Kit

After you send the master tape and the artwork off to have your CDs manufactured and assembled, there are several other things you need to take care of in order to prepare for the release. First, you need to make a press kit. A press kit is, just as its name implies, a kit of information that you send to members of the press in order to introduce them to you and your new record and to entice them to write about it.

A typical press kit consists of several components: a band photo, a biography of the band, and copies of any significant press the band has received. Although many publicists will tell you that a high quality press kit is key to the success of your record, the fact is that most music writers ignore press kits unless they're really, really bad. So, you're goal should be to create a press kit that "doesn't suck", without spending a lot of money. Here are some rules to help you do just that:

Take A Good Photograph

Take a good band photo. There's no need to spend a lot of money on a professional photographer. Just find a friend who has a 35-mm camera and take some pictures in a couple different settings and poses. Get the rolls developed and pick one that doesn't make you look like a dork or a poseur. If you don't have a friend with a 35-mm camera, head down to the photography department at your local college or university. You should be able to find someone who'll shoot a few rolls for the price of the film.

Keep Your Bio Brief And Engaging

Keep your bio short and interesting. When an editor reads your bio, she's looking for information about you and your record that will be of interest to her readers. So don't fill your bio with a lot of uninteresting background information or (even worse) hype about your music. Instead, fill it with stories about how everyone in your band got arrested for playing in their underwear outside a local convent, or that your band name is Roumanian for "fishmonger". If you've already had some success releasing records or playing live, definitely mention that at some point in your bio. But remember to keep it brief, engaging, and hype-free.

Include Your Five Best Reviews, Or Don't

Your press kit should also include clippings of any relevant press you've received, but not more than four or five pages worth. For a professional presentation, it's best to put each clipping on its own page, along with the masthead (titlebar) of the publication and the date alongside it. If the clippings are small, you can probably fit two on the same page. When you first start out, you may very well not have any press whatsoever. That's fine, but be prepared to update your kit as you start to get some reviews.

Keep It Cheap, But Nice

Enclose your kit in a folder that's attractive but not expensive. I'm fond of the colored folders with the clear acetate cover page and the binder that holds three-hole-punched pages. These folders allow you to create your own "cover" page without having to print on the outside of the folder itself, which saves time and money and gives you the flexibility to change the cover design if you need or want to at some point down the road. A three-hole binder is probably a good idea, as it keeps the papers inside from sliding out when the kit is inevitably tossed across the room into the "wait-and-see" pile.

Don't Include

Don't include trinkets like lapel buttons or bumperstickers. Press people will dump these in the trash as soon as they open your package.

Don't include lists of other bands you've played with, even if they're big and famous. Most people find these lists tacky and amateurish.

Quote Sheets

Do include a list of five to eight quotes from reviews and stories that have been written about you, but only if they're either very positive quotes from highly reputable sources or outlandishly negative quotes that are so over-the-top bad that they might peek an editor's curiosity

Most people probably think it would be suicidal to include a quote that openly disparaged their music, but under the right circumstances, this approach can be very effective. Take the example of Larry Shaw. Once, early in his career, Larry was booed off a stage in Nashville for playing a song called "Thin Girl". Rather than forget about the incident, Larry wrote a song about it called "Nashville", which turned out to be the title track of his debut CD. When it came time to make the press kit for the record, Larry chose to make the story behind "Nashville" the centerpiece of the bio, which attracted the interest of editors all over the country and resulted in a slew of (very favorable) reviews.

Be Yourself, Only Better

Which brings us to the final and most important point to keep in mind while creating your press kit: have a sense of humor, or at least humanity. Music editors get an awful lot of press kits in a week. If you can create a package that brings a smile to their face, you're going to do well.

How To Make Friends And Influence People

Want to make friends and influence people in the record business? Here's how: make cool T-shirts and then give them away with your record. Nothing will induce people to listen to your record and take you seriously more than a cool T-shirt.

Because of this, I highly recommend that you consider making T-shirts to promote your upcoming release. You don't need to spend all that much money to make an effective shirt: something in a 50/50 cotton-polyester blend will do (although 100% cotton is preferable), with one color printing on one side of a black or white shirt. For a full-scale national release, you'll need about 300 shirts (enough to send one to each station that adds your record, each writer that reviews it, and anyone else you need to impress along the way). For a regional release, you can probably get by with 100 or so, although most T-shirt makers offer price breaks starting at 144.

In general, you want to spend less than $5 per shirt. This shouldn't be too hard if you stick to one or maybe two color printing on only one side of the shirt. When you're haggling with the T-shirt maker, keep in mind that it's a very competitive business (especially in warm weather climates) and they've usually got an extra dollar or two of profit built into their published prices.

As for what to put on the shirt, you might consider making a silk screen of the design from your album cover, if it's something that would reproduce well in a single color at lower resolution. (T-shirt screens have only about half the resolution of a typical paper printing press.) Otherwise, try to come up with a funny or memorable slogan that ties in with your band name, album name, or some other element of your press kit. (This is one of those places where it's nice to have a marketable album name.) For example, the first Huge T-shirt featured a picture of the lead singer as a three-year-old taken from the album cover with a heading that read: "Huge—he's getting bigger..."

At this point, you're probably sitting there thinking: "You want me to give away $1,200 worth of T-shirts for free?" Yes. That's exactly what I want you to do, and here's why. That $1,200 investment is probably going to do more to distinguish your product from your competition than anything else you can do. You may be the greatest performer in the history of music, but it isn't gonna matter one bit if you can't get anyone to listen to your record. There's no doubt about it, T-shirts are expensive. They're so expensive that almost no one includes them with their packages. And that's why yours is going to stand out.

A typical college radio station might receive one hundred records in a single week. If you send them a package with just a CD and a press kit, no matter how professional, it's just going to be tossed into the pile with all the others. But if your package also contains a cool T-shirt...well, that's a whole different story.

Chapter 6

How It's All Going To Work

You've got 2,500 CDs in boxes at the foot of your bed; you've assembled an entertaining and informative press kit containing a band photo that's not the least bit dorky; and you've found a surfer in San Diego who will silkscreen your two color promo T-shirts for $3.50 a piece.

Finally, you're ready for the release. Well, almost. There's one more thing you're going to need before you begin your meteoric rise to superstardom, and that's: a plan.

The Real Work Is Just Beginning

While it probably seems like you've come to the end of a long and winding road, which will soon bring you fame, love, and untold riches, in fact, the really hard work is just about to begin. In order to be successful, you need to sit down right now and decide exactly what it is you're trying to accomplish, and how you're going to accomplish it.

We've made this point before, but it definitely bears repeating: *making records and selling records are two completely different activities.* In order to make a great record, you need to think like a musician. In order to sell a lot of records, you need to think like a businessperson. And one thing that good businesspeople do is plan how they are going to carry out their business.

Three Steps To Success

Selling is, on its most fundamental level, a three step process. To start with, you need a product—preferably a good one—to sell. Hopefully, you've already taken care of this step. Second, you need to find or create a way to make your product available for sale to the public. And lastly, you need to make the public aware that your product exists, and convince them that they absolutely need to have it. If you can do these three things, you will succeed, and that's really about all there is to it.

Most indie bands/artists have two problems with this strategy. The first is that they find it abhorrent to think of their lovingly crafted music as a "product", to be bought and sold like so much fish. The second is that those who are more than willing to get out there and sell their music have no idea how or where to start. We'll fix the second problem in a few minutes. Right now, it's the first problem I want to talk about.

Music Is A Product

It's unfortunate that so many indie artists think it's evil to treat music as a product to be bought and sold. For one thing, whether you like it or not, music *is* a product to be bought and sold (to the tune of $12 billion last year in record sales alone). And it's a good thing it is, because if it weren't you would have very little chance of making a living as a musician.

There's no doubt that life at the big record labels, retailers, and radio stations involves a lot of what you'd probably consider ethical compromise (not to mention flat-out corruption). But there's also no doubt that it's the activities of these businesses that allow honest and creative people like you to make their living playing music. Music is a product, and it happens to be one that millions of people are willing and eager to pay for. And because it is, more music—and more different kinds of music—are being made (and more musicians are being paid) than ever before.

And another thing: just because a CD is a product for sale does not mean that it can't also be a beautiful, emotional form of expression. In fact, many of the best selling records are also breathtaking artistic achievements. I'm not suggesting that you need to think of your record as a product and *not* an artistic expression; I'm suggesting that you'll have more success (and probably more artistic satisfaction) if you think of your record as an artistic expression that is *also* a product that must be effectively distributed, promoted, and sold if you are going to have a career.

The Plan

Hopefully, I've convinced you that you're not selling yourself down the river by deciding to run your business like a businessperson. If I haven't, well… at least they can't say I didn't try.

So how does one sell records like a businessperson? Let's go back to that three-step plan. For those of you who don't recall, the three step-plan for selling anything is: make it, distribute it, promote it.

Hopefully, you've already made a great record. Your next step (arguably the most difficult) is to line up solid distribution. Once you've got distribution, you're going to promote yourself and your record via the radio, the music press, and live shows.

You will start by distributing and promoting your record locally, even if you have the talent, the desire, and the budget to reach a national audience. You will "build a buzz" by using success in one area of promotion (say, radio airplay) to create successes in others (live shows, press coverage, etc.) in an endless, upward spiral.

You will then use the foundation of success you establish locally to expand the scope of your distribution and promotion to other cities, other states, other regions, and maybe even other countries. At all times, you will manage your cash flow and inventory wisely, you will be creative, resourceful, professional, and doggedly persistent. You will find and expand the market for your music by understanding and ignoring the conventions used by others. And hopefully, you'll have the time of your life.

Why Start Small?

Those of you who are planning to go national with your release might wonder why it's best to start locally and build outward. After all, when the major labels have a hit record on their hands, they don't mess around with local promotions, do they? Well, yes, actually they do, except in cases where the band in question has already established itself as a national act (we're talking a minimum of 200,000 records sold here).

If you've already sold 200,000 records, then by all means, go national right away, if that's what's going to make you happy. But those of you who haven't yet sold 200,000 records are going to need to start locally. There are several advantages to this strategy. For one thing, it's do-able. Remember, before you can promote your record, you need to get good distribution in the area of the promotion (or else why bother promoting it?) Suffice it to say that as an unknown band with few or no verifiable record sales, you are not going to be able to get even decent national distribution no matter how great your record sounds, and that's just a fact. Mail-order does not constitute effective distribution (except in very rare cases), and even if it did, it wouldn't matter, because no radio station or magazine outside your local area is going to pay attention to you if you don't have a local (or even regional) buzz behind you.

So you're going to start locally, and that's great. Because the local level is the perfect place to learn the principles you're going to apply on a larger scale at some point down the road: it's easier to get distribution on a local level; there are fewer stores to stock, which means less product to ship and fewer store-owners to keep happy; there are fewer radio stations and music publications to promote to, so you can afford to be a bit more elaborate in your promotions and you'll have an easier time developing personal relationships with music directors, DJs, editors, and writers; all the clubs will be close to your home, so you won't have to drive very far to promote and play shows; because you're local, you should have an easier time getting retail space, radio airplay, and definitely press coverage. And most importantly, when you do decide to branch out to other markets, you'll have "a story" to tell that will grab the attention of people who have never heard of you.

Chapter 7

Meet The Players

Over the course of this release, you're going to be meeting and dealing with a lot of different people and companies. In order to make the most of your interactions with them, you need to understand who they are and what they do. The groups you need to be familiar with are: distributors, retailers, radio, and the press.

Distributors

Distributors are in the business of distributing records. They don't make records, and they don't sell them. They distribute them; which is to say, they move them from place to place—specifically, back and forth between record labels and retailers. In return for moving them, and for keeping track of all the related accounting, distributors receive a portion of the revenue generated—typically about 20-25% of the wholesale price—by those records that "sell through" to end consumers.

There are several different kinds of distributors, but the two you need to be familiar with are national independent distributors (which we'll call "national indies") and "one-stops". National indie distributors make most of their money by distributing the records of large independent record labels to regional and national retail record chains. One-stops, on the other hand, specialize in providing a complete selection of records from a wide variety of labels both large and small to standalone independent record stores known as "mom-and-pop" stores. They're called one-stops because they provide "one-stop shopping" to buyers from these stores.

Be it a national indie or a one-stop, a distributor gets paid by a retailer when they ship records to that retailer (or at least, within sixty days of when they ship the records), with the agreement that if the records don't sell, the retailer can return them for a full refund or credit. If the records "sell through" (i.e., if customers buy them), the distributor then pays the record labels that provided those records— *starting with the labels that are most critical to the distributor's business.*

Because distributors only make money on records that actually sell through, they're much more inclined to work with record labels that have the resources, experience, and clout necessary to promote their records effectively. Most national indie distributors have sales-people who "sell" the distributor's records to buyers from retail record chains. If the buyer agrees to carry a particular record, the retailer will order some copies (called "units" or "pieces") of that record, and place them in the retailer's central warehouse, where they will be available to any of the stores in the chain that want to stock them. They will also enter the record into their computerized accounting system, which facilitates the ordering process.

Once the records have been shipped to the warehouse and entered into the computer system, it is the responsibility of both the record label and the distributor to convince the individual stores in the chain to stock the record. As I mentioned earlier in the section on major labels, this job is called retail marketing and how well you do it can make or break your career. (We'll discuss your role in the marketing process in greater detail a little bit later.)

To summarize, it's the distributor's job to make your record available to individual record stores. It's *your* job to help the distributor convince those stores to order it.

Retailers

Retailers, also known as record stores, come in a variety of shapes and sizes ranging from mom-and-pops to mega-chains like Tower, Blockbuster, Wherehouse and Musicland/SamGoody. Retailers make much of their money by selling records to end consumers, but as we discussed earlier, they also make a sizeable portion of their income by renting their shelf space to record labels in the form of retail advertising.

Due to the effect of advertising, a large retailer can actually make more money on a slow-selling major label release than on a popular indie record. Needless to say, this makes things more difficult for indie labels and indie artists. To make matters worse, several of the large national retail chains are in the process of buying up mom-and-pop stores and smaller chains as a way of increasing their leverage with labels, distributors, and the buying public. As regional retail chains disappear, so too do the regional distributors that supply them. The result is higher retail prices, lower wholesale prices, fewer sales of indie records, fewer indie labels, and fewer successful indie bands.

Radio

Community Radio Stations

Community radio stations, also called public stations, get their funding from donations made by local listeners and businesses. Community stations are typically non-profit organizations licensed by the Federal Communications Commission (FCC) to serve a particular broadcasting need in the community. As a result, they often feature foreign-language shows, National Public Radio, and other talk-based specialty programming. Those community stations that do play music typically play a wide variety of styles, in blocks of 2-4 hours per style.

Cable-Current Stations

Cable-current stations are college stations (and sometimes high school stations) that broadcast their signals through phone lines. In order to receive a signal from a cable-current station, the listener must take her phone off the hook, point her antenna toward the phone, and sometimes even wrap her phone cord around the antenna. Needless to say, the signals broadcasted by these stations are often very weak, and do not reach a wide audience.

Cable Stations

Cable stations are non-profit organizations that broadcast music behind news and weather channels on cable TV stations. While cable stations are often very receptive to playing music by unknown artists, they tend to have very small audiences.

College Radio

College radio stations get most if not all of their funding from the college or university with which they are affiliated. As a result, their primary mission is to fulfill the listening needs of that university community. They tend to play more music than public stations, and the music they play tends to be less diverse, focusing mainly on college rock or hip-hop, depending on the make-up of the community.

Not all college radio stations are created equal. Some stations reach much wider audiences than others, and have a much greater impact on local record sales. These high-impact stations are called "priority" stations, and they're the ones you're going to be targeting in your release. We'll go into more detail about college radio stations and how they work when we get to the section on radio promotion.

Commercial Radio

As we discussed earlier, commercial radio stations are corporations that play music as a way to attract listeners that they can then "deliver" to advertisers in return for money. The more listeners they attract, the more money they make. Unlike other types of stations, commercial stations are not concerned with meeting the needs of the community. They're concerned with keeping their ratings high and selling advertising, and experience has taught them that the best way to do that is to target listeners of a particular type, or "demographic", and play the music that most appeals to them.

Fortunately for radio stations and their advertisers, it so happens that most people in the same demographic are drawn to the same kind of music. For example, suburban white males between the ages of 18 and 24 tend to like "alternative" rock while urban black females between 14 and 21 tend to prefer R&B.

In radio-speak, these different styles of music are called "formats". Common formats include AOR (album oriented rock—bands like Soul Asylum and Pearl Jam), CHR (chart hit rock—"Top 40" artists like Michael Bolton and Mariah Carey), Urban (hip-hop and R&B), "Churban" (a combination of CHR and Urban), AC (adult contemporary—pop artists like Billy Joel and Sting), AAA (album adult alternative—singer/songwriter and folksy-rock acts like Eric Clapton and Cheryl Crow), Modern Rock ("alternative" artists like Green Day, Alanis Morissette, and Oasis), and Jazz.

As a rule, DJs at commercial stations have very little (if any) say in which records they play on their shows, and program directors for these stations will not add a record by a new artist unless that record has already established an impressive record of audience acceptance at both college and other commercial stations. Needless to say, getting an independent record added on a commercial station is not easy, but it's not impossible if you're persistent and you know what you're doing.

Press

Fanzines

Like radio stations and retailers, music publications come in many different shapes and sizes. The main types you need to worry about are fanzines, college newspapers, alternative newsweeklies, metropolitan newspapers, and music magazines. Fanzines are small journals dedicated to a particular style of music, or in some cases, a particular band. They are usually written, compiled, and edited by a single person, typically a high school or college student. Compared to other types of publications, fanzines are published less frequently and less consistently and have smaller readerships (usually less than 2,000). Fanzines are usually very open to covering new music, as long as it fits the general vibe of the 'zine.

E-zines

Recently there has emerged a new kind of fanzine called an "e-zine" (short for "electronic magazine"), which is distributed electronically over the World Wide Web (WWW). Because e-zines are cheap and relatively easy to create and distribute, they'll no doubt become increasingly popular in the years to come. And because they're delivered electronically, they can offer their readers a feature no other music publication can—the ability to download samples of the music they're writing about. If you want to learn more about e-zines, a good place to start is a WWW directory like Yahoo (the URL for Yahoo's music section is "http://www.yahoo.com/Entertainment/Music").

College Newspapers

College newspapers, like college radio stations, receive most of their funding from their affiliated college or university, and are chartered to serve the needs of their academic community. Fortunately, most college kids value new music, so most college newspapers give it broad coverage, in terms of both record reviews and announcements of upcoming shows.

When a new record comes into a college news room, the music editor usually puts it into a box labeled "for review", where it is available to any of the staff music writers who want to review it. If a writer wants to review (or steal) the record, he'll take it home and listen to it. If you're lucky, he'll write a review and submit it to the music editor for publication. If you're not he won't, and there isn't much you can do about it unless you can give the paper a compelling reason to run the review—e.g., go there to play a show, or take out an advertisement in the paper.

Alternative Newsweeklies

Alternative newsweeklies provide coverage for news, art, and entertainment stories that fall outside the realm of the mainstream media. Although they're called newsweeklies, they're often published every other week, and are found mostly in urban areas, where they are distributed for free on street corners and in record stores and cafes. A group called the Assocation of Alternative Newsweeklies (AAN) maintains a directory of all the major alternative newsweeklies in the U.S., which you can obtain for free by calling (602) 229-8487. This directory is updated every year, and it's enormously helpful in planning your press campaign, so call today and have them send you one.

In keeping with their identity as "alternative" media outlets, newsweeklies are more receptive than daily newspapers to "alternative" forms of music like acid jazz, experimental rock, and spoken word. The writers and editors at newsweeklies don't work there for the money. (Many are so underpaid they have to take second jobs to keep food on the table.) They work there because they believe in the cause and importance of the alternative media. Of all the people you'll deal with over the course of your release, these folks will be some of the most supportive of what you're doing. So be nice to them—they're on your side.

Daily newspapers

Almost every city with a population above 100,000 people has a daily newspaper. Most of these newspapers give fairly sizeable coverage to new record releases, reviews of performances, and announcements of upcoming events. Compared to alternative newsweeklies, college newspapers, and fanzines, daily newspapers tend to be more conservative in what types of music they cover and how they cover them. Instead of hiring their own record reviewers, many smaller dailies run syndicated reviews taken from larger metropolitan papers.

Larger papers vary dramatically in their attitudes toward covering local music. Some have weekly columns devoted to up-and-coming bands while others won't mention a band unless they're already signed to a major label. But many daily papers provide coverage to independent bands that come from out of town to play a show, especially if they've scheduled other promotional tie-ins like college radio interviews and in-store performances.

Keep in mind that if you grew up in one town and then moved to another to begin your music career, you'll probably be able to persuade your hometown newspaper to run a "local boy/girl made good" story about you when you release your first record, with follow-ups as your career ascends to new heights. Aside from being a very wise business move, this one will pay big dividends when it comes time for your high school reunion.

National Music Magazines

National music magazines cover new music and "culture" on a national level. The larger nationals, like "Spin" and "Rolling Stone", tend to be more corporate in their approach, and less accessible to independent musicians with limited promotional budgets. But smaller magazines like "Option" and "Alternative Press" do occasionally run reviews of self-released records.

National Music Trades

We covered the national music trade publications in depth during our discussion of major label releases, so rather than repeat myself, I'll just hit the highlights here.

Trade journals are published for the benefit of people in the music industry, specifically the music and program directors at college and commercial radio stations. The main trades you need to be familiar with are the *College Music Journal (CMJ)*, *Gavin*, *Friday Morning Quarterback (FMQB)*, *Album Network*, *Hard Report*, *Radio & Records (R&R)*, *Hits*, and *Billboard*. As I mentioned in our earlier discussion, each of these trades maintains charts for the different radio formats of their readers. *CMJ* and *Gavin* are targeted toward college and smaller commercial stations. *FMQB*, *Album Network*, and *Hard Report* are aimed at small and medium-size commercial stations. *R&R*, *Hits* and *Billboard* cover larger commercial stations.

If you aren't familiar with these publications (and I can't think of a reason why you should be), I highly recommend that you get a copy of each and read through them. (You'll probably be appalled to see how music is packaged and sold to the people at radio.) You might be able to find some of them, like *CMJ* and *Billboard*, at your local library or record store. To get the others, call the publications themselves and tell them you're considering buying advertising. They should be more than happy to send you a free sample copy.

Chapter 8

Planning The Release

In this chapter, you're going to complete the three tasks necessary to prepare for your initial release:

1. Pick your homebase market.
2. Establish your "suggested retail price" or SRP.
3. Gather names/addresses/etc. of the people and organizations involved in Phase One of the release.

Success Begins At Home

The first thing you need to do in planning your release is to pick the city ("market") that will serve as your home base. This is the city where you will first launch the record and begin to build your "story" of success. Because of this, the city you pick for your home base must be large enough to support significant record sales and close enough to your home that you can travel there easily to promote and play shows and meet with people at radio, retail, and the press.

In general, you want to pick a home base that has a population of at least 300,000 people and is no more than thirty minutes' drive from your home. If your situation is such that you don't live within thirty minutes of a city this size, I strongly suggest you consider moving. I know this is a lot to ask, and of course the choice is entirely up to you. But remember that your entire strategy for the release is to build a buzz locally and then use that initial success as leverage to expand into larger markets. In order for this strategy to work, you have to *have* an initial success on which to build, and it has to be big enough to make people in other areas sit up and take notice.

In addition to being big enough and close enough to you, your home base needs to have at least a moderately-sized market for the type of music you make. For example, if you're a modern rock band and you live in Houston, you probably know there isn't much of a market for modern rock in your hometown. You might have better luck in a city like Dallas.

How can you tell if the city nearest you has a reasonable market for your style of music? First, check out the commercial radio stations. If there's at least one "major" commercial station in your city that plays music in your format, that's a good sign. Then, check out your local clubs. Will there be anywhere for you to play in support of your release? Do you see major label acts of your general type playing shows in your area? If so, that's another good sign. If you're still in doubt, check out the record stores—do they devote a significant amount of shelf space to your style of music? Talk to the record store managers and ask them about sales in your style. And last but not least, read the local music papers. Do they devote coverage to your style of music? Do you see stories of bands from your area that have built successful careers and/or caught the attention of the major labels? Again, if you're not where you need to be, this is the time to consider moving.

Establishing Your 'SRP'

Once you've selected an appropriate home base for your release, the next thing you need to do is establish the "suggested retail price" (SRP). Obviously, the retail price of your "product" is going to depend on what kind of product it is. If you've taken my advice up to this point, you've created an LP length CD. Typically, major label LPCDs have an SRP between $13.99 and $15.98.

If you've ever taken a class in economics (or if you have a little common sense) you know that if you charge more for your CD, you'll make more money per CD, but you'll sell fewer copies. If you charge less, you'll make less per CD, but you'll sell more copies.

Because of this, the price you choose for your CD can have a big impact on both sales and profits. So it's important to choose well.

I recommend that you go with an SRP of $11.98. In my opinion, this price is high enough that you can make some money (your share after distribution will be about $6.00) but low enough that many record buyers who aren't very familiar with your music will be willing to "take a chance" on your record.

One of the most common mistakes I see among indie bands is that they charge too much for their records. Remember, mall chain stores *and independent record stores* are probably going to add as much as two dollars to your suggested retail price, so if your SRP is $14.99, your record could easily cost as much as $16.99 on the street. At this point, you've got to ask yourself: would you pay $16.99 for a record by a band you'd barely heard of? Probably not, and neither would most other people. Don't be greedy—$11.98.

Filling Your Database

Once you've picked your home base and established your SRP, your next job is to track down all the address and contact information you're going to need for Phase One of the release. This is where you're going to start making use of that database software you purchased back in Chapter Four while you were setting up your home office.

You're going to be calling on the information in this database constantly over the course of the next few months and years, so it's very important that you set up your database program correctly from the start. You do *not* want to have to re-enter two thousand names, addresses, and phone numbers.

Regardless of which database program you use, you need to be able to do the following things. First, you absolutely must have the ability to record at least one phone number, one fax number, and one email address for each contact in your database. (If you're not using email now, I promise that you (and everyone else) will be sometime in the next three years, so plan accordingly.) In addition, you must have the ability to separate and call up contacts on the basis of their "category", e.g. radio, press, distributor reps, retail, fan club, and live show mailing list. If you use a program like ACT 2.0, Touchbase, or FileMaker Pro, you can register a single person as belonging to multiple categories. This is nice because it saves you from having to make double entries for press people who are also on your mailing list, etc. Last but not least, you need to be able to print mailing labels for these different groups after you've separated them.

One other thing that's nice to have (and comes standard in packages like ACT and Touchbase) is the ability to make notes of your conversations with each of the contacts in your database. Depending on how comfortable you are using the computer (and on how good your memory is) this can be a great asset in maintaining your business relationships.

Make Regular Back-Ups Of Your Data

But regardless of which program you use and how you configure it, there's one thing you absolutely must do, and that's *make regular back-up copies of your data!* I cannot emphasize this point strongly enough. You're going to spend a lot time and energy compiling the information in this database, and some of it is going to be irreplaceable if you lose it. Take my word for it—your hard disk *will* fail Your floppy disk *will* get stepped on or lost. So protect yourself by copying your data file onto a second computer or some other back-up medium every month. It's also a good idea to make a hard copy (i.e., print it out on paper) every six months. I know it's a pain, but if and when your system goes down, you'll be very *very* glad you did.

Gathering The Information: Distributors

Once you've got your database program all configured and you've sworn on your mother's honor to make regular back-ups, it's time to start compiling the information you're going to need for Phase One of your release. First, you need to get the names and phone/fax numbers of all the independent distributors that supply records of your style to stores in and around your home base. You should be able to obtain a list of these distributors from the *Recording Industry Sourcebook* (aka "*The Sourcebook*") or *The Yellow Pages of Rock* (*YPR*). If you don't already own a recent copy of one of these two directories, now would be an excellent time to get one—you can buy a copy of *The Sourcebook* by calling (800) 233-9604; the number for *YPR* is (818) 955-4000. (Don't be surprised when they answer the phone "Album Network...")

Call each distributor on your list to find out the name of the person in charge of signing up new record labels, and verify that the distributor carries your style of music in your area.

Radio

Next, you need to compile a list of all the commercial, college, high school, and community radio stations that broadcast music of your style to your home base, complete with the names, phone numbers, fax numbers, and email addresses of the music and/or program directors (whoever it is that decides which records get added to the playlist for that station). The stations don't need to be dedicated entirely to your style of music, but they need to broadcast at least five to ten hours of it per week (and preferably to more than a handful of people) in order to be of interest to you. When you call the college and commercial stations, it might also be a good idea to find out which trades, if any, they report their playlist to—this will give you an indication of the size of the station's listening audience.

You can get a list of commercial stations from *YPR* or the music trades. You can get the college, high school and community station info from the directory put out by *CMJ*.

Beware! The music and program directors, and even the addresses, of college radio stations are constantly changing. No matter how up-to-date your information is, you should *always* call to confirm this information before sending records or other material.

Press

Next you're going to need names, addresses, and phone/fax numbers for all the local press outlets in your home base market.

This includes fanzines, college (and maybe high school) newspapers, weekly neighborhood newspapers, alternative newsweeklies, and daily newspapers. You can probably find most of this information at your local newsstand or library. You might also want to check out your local indie record store and ask the sales clerks there if they know of any local fanzines that might be of interest to you.

Retail

Next, you need to find out where the people who listen to music of your type go to buy records. You can usually do this by asking the folks at your local college radio stations. You can also find some of this information in the *CMJ* directory and *YPR*. Be sure to get the name, phone/fax number, and calling hours of the "buyer" for every store on your list. These are the people you need to convince to stock your record.

Clubs And Other Venues

Finally, this is a good time to make a list of all the venues where you might conceivably perform in order to promote your new release. When you call clubs, be sure to get the name of the person who screens the packages, and verify whether it's okay to send them on CD. Unbelievably, a lot of these people don't own CD players, and can only accept tapes. Also, be sure to find out their policy with regard to scheduling shows; i.e., How soon can you start calling them? Some "talent buyers" have a strict "don't call us, we'll call you" policy—this is annoying, but it's better to know in advance.

Remember, there are a lot of places you can play beside clubs. In fact, playing an alternate venue will often result in more exposure than playing a club because of the novelty of the event. Alternate venues you should consider include local record stores, high schools, churches and synagogues, street fairs, etc. For more ideas in this vein, check out the events calendar of your daily and neighborhood newspapers.

Also, this is a good time to start keeping an eye out for major label (and popular indie) acts that are going to be playing in your area. One great way to get exposure and build your buzz is to open for a more well-known act with a built-in draw. If you know who's coming well in advance, you can suggest yourself to the club's talent buyer as an opening act for specific shows, which dramatically increases your chances of getting booked.

Chapter 9

Distribution

Getting Some

Now we're ready for step two of the selling process: distribution. "Getting distribution" means developing and maintaining a profitable business relationship with a quality distributor. Most musicians I meet think getting good distribution is impossible. The truth is, it's not easy to convince a quality distributor to carry your records and stock them in sufficient quantity; but it's *definitely not impossible* if you know what you're doing and you're willing to do some work.

How It Works

Before we get into the nitty-gritty of getting and maintaining good distribution, I want to give you a general overview of how it's all going to work. First, you're going to create what's called a "one-sheet"—a one-page description of your record that tells distributors and retailers why they should carry it. Next, you're going to mail packages containing your record along with the one-sheet to the distributors in your area. Then—this is the hard part—you're going to meet with them, either by phone or in person, and convince them to work with you.

If/once you find a distributor who wants to work with you (and with whom you feel comfortable), you'll enter into a business relationship with them by signing a distribution agreement, which is a short contract that outlines the terms and conditions of your business arrangement. At this point, the distributor will send you a purchase order, or "P.O.", for some records. You'll ship the records, and the distributor will try to convince stores within the area of your promotion to stock them.

The distributor will handle all the accounting, and will pay you for the records either when they need more records from you or when you decide to "recall" the release. If they need more records, they'll send you another P.O., and you'll ship them more records. If things go smoothly, you'll find yourself in a state of "dynamic equilibirium", in which you're shipping records (by your band and maybe others as well) to the distributor and in return the distributor is paying you for past shipments that have already sold at retail. The more records you have that the distributor wants, and the more copies of these records that are being ordered by retailers, the more attention you'll get from (and the faster you'll be paid by) the distributor.

Sound easy enough? Good. Let's give it a try!

The One-Sheet

The first step is to create the "one-sheet" for your release. Recall from above that the purpose of the one-sheet is to convince distributors and retailers to stock your record, and to give them all the information they need to enter it into their computerized accounting systems. (Beware: if your distributor is not using a computerized accounting and tracking system, they probably won't be able to keep track of where they've shipped your records or find out how many have sold.)

Your one-sheet should be printed on your label letterhead, and should include the following information centered near the top of the page:

Artist name:
Name of release:
Label name:
Date of release:
UPC (bar code) #:
Selection #:
Suggested Retail Price:

Below this information should be a brief description of the record and the band, highlighting those points that will contribute to record sales. For example, if there are specific tracks that are likely to be embraced by college radio, list them. If your lead singer has a distinctive voice, describe it. If your lead guitarist is a twelve year-old immigrant from mainland China, mention that. As always, keep the hype to a minimum.

In addition to describing the aspects of the music that will help it sell, talk briefly about the promotion of the record. In your case, you should mention that you're going to launch the record locally, in conjunction with a promotion to college and community radio, and local press, and that you'll be playing a series of live shows and other promotional events. If you happen to have some quality gigs lined up already, mention them. Mention briefly your plans to expand the promotion. Do you plan to tour regionally or nationally in support of the record? If so, how many dates and where are you planning to play?

The Mail-Out

Once you've completed the one-sheet, you're ready for the mail-out. First, go to your local copy store and make 100 copies each of your bio and your one-sheet (you're going to need some extras to send to the distributor reps later on). Then, go to the post-office and pick up 25 of the big, floppy Priority Mail envelopes, and 25 of the smaller cardboard Priority Mail envelopes. (Be sure you don't accidentally grab the Express Mail envelopes—they cost four times as much to send.) While you're there, you might as well buy 100 priority mail stamps; it will save you some trips in the future.

Once you've got your supplies together, use your database program to call up the names and addresses of the indie distributors and one-stops in your area, and print mailing labels for them. This will tell you how many packages you need to assemble. For each distributor on your list, place a CD, a bio, and a one-sheet into a cardboard envelope, seal the envelope, and place it into one of the bigger floppy envelopes. Then seal the floppy envelope and label it with both the shipping address and your return address. (This is where it's nice to have those shipping labels with your name and logo on them.) When you've got all the packages assembled, take them down to the post office and mail them. If you've already got the postage on the envelopes when you take them to the post office, you can usually go around to the back and drop them off without having to stand in line.

Getting Noticed

Why use two envelopes? Wouldn't it be easier and more environmentally-friendly to just put the stuff in the cardboard envelope and send it that way? Sure. But your goal is not just to get the stuff to the distributor—it's to get it there in a form that will grab the distributor's attention.

Imagine for a minute that you're a distributor. It's Monday morning and you've arrived at the office to find twenty packages sitting on your desk. Nineteen of them are plain paper envelopes from labels you've never heard of, and one of them is a big, floppy, red-white-and-blue Priority Mail envelope, from a label that faxed you the day before to warn you it was coming. Which one would you open? Remember, you're competing with a lot of other people for the attention of that distributor... the bigger and more colorful your envelope is, the better your chances are that he'll open it. Why not just use the big, floppy envelopes then, and forget about the cardboard ones? For one thing, the cardboard envelopes protect the contents of the package. For another, the distributor is more likely to remember a package that required him to open two envelopes. And for another, they're free.

The Fax Can Be Used Like A Knife

The day after you mail out the packages, go back to your database program and output the fax numbers of all the distributors on your list. (You should be able to have the program do this for you automatically, using some kind of "export" command.) Then, if you have a computer fax/modem, input the names and fax numbers of your distributors into your fax software (this you'll probably have to do by hand), so that you can fax everyone on your list in a single "batch".

After you've gotten everything squared away with the fax software, use your word processor to make a one-page letter that briefly explains who you are and what you're trying to accomplish. Mention that you're looking for distribution and that you'll call in three days to discuss the matter. When you're done, fax it to all the distributors on your list, preferably with a customized fax cover sheet that you can create in your fax program itself.

A New Kind Of Relationship

Now it's time to start calling the distributors. But before you do, this would be a good time to take a step back and think about exactly what it is you're trying to accomplish.

Up to this point, you've been a customer of other businesses: you bought studio time; you hired a graphic designer; you had CDs pressed. In all these cases, you paid money and received a product or service in return. At this point, the studio where you made your record has no financial stake in the success of your release because, no matter what happens, they've already been paid. The same is true of the graphic designer and the CD manufacturer.

But the relationship you're hoping to establish with your distributor... that's a different story. In this case, you're not going to be a customer of the distributor, you're going to be a business partner. You're not going to pay up-front for services rendered, you're going to ship your records to the distributor and he's going to ship them to retailers, and he's only going to get paid if your records sell through.

In other words, for the first time (but not the last) in your budding business career, you're going to ask someone to do something for you without offering to pay him in advance. And why will he agree to help you? Because you're going to convince him that over the long-haul he's going to make a lot of money by doing so. And the way you're going to do *that* is by telling him your "story".

Your Story

Your "story" is the brief narrative that describes where you've been, where you are, and where you're going. It's a thirty second monologue in which you chart the course of your business and your career in a way that subtly screams "Hey, look at me! I'm not like all the other bozos you have to talk to all day long. I know what I'm doing. I know where I want to go, and I know how to get there."

Your story is not hype. It's a calm, self-assured, honest description of what you've accomplished and what you have planned, with a healthy dose of optimism. Right now, your story might go something like this:

> "Hi, my name is Dave. I represent a band called
> The Self-Fulfilled Prophets. We've been together for
> two years and we've built up a solid following in
> the San Francisco area. Now we're preparing to
> release our first full-length CD. We're going to start
> the release locally with a full-scale promotion to
> college radio and the press, and a series of shows at
> Slim's, The Paradise Lounge, and Great American
> Music Hall. From there, we're going to build the
> release to the rest of California, the West Coast, and
> eventually the entire U.S., with a national tour
> scheduled for the fall."

Of course, it helps if you already have some solid accomplishments on which to build your story. But *how* you tell your story can sometimes be even more important than what you have to say. If you make it clear that you know what you're doing and you're willing to work hard, people will respond well to you, even if it's clear that you're just starting out. (Hey, everyone has to start sometime.)

So get your story together now. Go over it with your bandmates and friends. Rehearse it in the mirror with a phone up to your ear. Call up your mom and explain to her one more time "exactly what it is you think you're doing." If you're like most people, you'll feel awkward at first. But over time, you'll get better at it and you'll feel more comfortable. And the next thing you know, you'll be having power lunches with major label presidents. (Don't laugh, it could happen.)

Making The Calls

About three to five days after you send the records, call up each of the distributors on your list. First, ask them if they *got* the package ("...the one that came in the big Priority Mail envelope"). If they didn't get it or they don't remember it, tell them you'll send another (and then send it!). If they got the package, ask them whether they've had a chance to listen to it. If they haven't listened to it yet, tell them your story—i.e., briefly explain what you're looking for in terms of distribution (presence in local stores, expanding outward to other cities and regions) and what you're planning to do for the promotion (radio promotion, press coverage, live shows, etc.)—and ask them to listen to it in the next week.

If you can't get anyone on the phone, leave a brief but detailed voice-mail message containing the information in the above paragraph, and tell them you'll call back the next day. If you can't reach anyone after three days or so, send them a fax containing the information and asking them to call you. If they don't call after about three more days, send another fax, repeating the information and asking them how you can get in touch with them ("When is a good time to call?") If, after three or four weeks, you haven't been able to speak to a real human being, cross them off your list—at least for now.

If you do manage to get someone on the phone who has actually listened to your record, ask him how he liked it. If he didn't hate it, tell him what you want for distribution and what you're going to do for promotion, and ask him if he's interested. If he is, he'll want to know the SRP (I suggest $11.98) and the wholesale price (usually 47-50% of the SRP; I suggest $6.00).

Some bands try to get cute and ask for a wholesale price of $7 instead of $6. What usually happens in this case is that the distributor agrees to the higher price, and then sells the records to the retailers for $9-10; the retailers, in turn, price the records at $13.99, with mall stores charging as much as $15.98.

To put it another way: raising your wholesale price by one dollar can raise the price of your record at retail by as much as two or three dollars. So don't be greedy: ask for an SRP of $11.98 and a wholesale price of $6.

What You Want

Your goal is to find a distributor who will take enough copies of your record to cover the stores in the area of your promotion, which for the time being is your home base city. Ask your distributor how many records he'll take in his initial order. Hopefully, he'll want to take at least fifty. If he wants to take fewer than twenty-five, you're probably better off looking elsewhere. Whatever you do, don't enter into an exclusive distribution agreement (i.e., one that prevents you from doing business with other distributors) with a distributor that won't take enough records to provide you with sufficient retail coverage.

You'll also need to negotiate the payment terms. Keep in mind that most distributors aren't going to pay you on time unless your record is selling consistently and/or you have more releases coming out that are of interest to them. The payment terms you want are "net 60", which means the distributor must pay you no more than sixty days after you send him an invoice (i.e., the bill). Some distributors will ask for a 2% discount in return for paying within sixty days. This is referred to as "2% net 60". If your distributor asks for such a discount, tell him you find this unacceptable, and suggest "net 60" instead. (Why should he get a discount just for paying on time?)

Your distributor is also going to want to include a clause in the contract that guarantees him the right to return any unsold or damaged records for a full refund or credit. Unfortunately, this has become standard industry practice, so there's no way out of this one. The bottom line is this: if you can get your foot in the door with a quality distributor who's willing to take a reasonable number of your records, and who can grow with you over time, you're doing very, very well.

If At First You Don't Succeed

If after a month or two you can't find a good distributor who'll take a decent number of records, don't despair and don't take it personally. This is a very tough time for distributors, and most of them are doing all they can just to keep their heads above water. The fact that you can't get them to work with you (or maybe even return your phone calls) now does *not* mean that you won't be able to get through to them later.

So, if you've given it your all and you still don't have distribution, the best thing to do is to go ahead with the release anyway. You should be able to get some local stores to take your record on consignment (see below), which will get you through Phase One of the release. Once you start playing shows and getting radio airplay (and maybe even selling some records), you can go back to the distributors again and try to line up distribution for the later phases of the campaign, when it will be more critical.

Once You've Signed The Agreement

After you sign an agreement with your distributor, they'll send you a purchase order (or "P.O.") for some records. The purchase order is the distributor's way of saying, "We agree to purchase X quantity of the following record, and to pay by such-and-such a date."

I recommend that you start a new folder in your filing cabinet called "Distributor Docs". Into this folder, you should place subfolders called "Contracts" and "Outstanding P.O.s". Put your distribution agreement into the first file and the P.O. into the second one. I know this level of organization probably seems excessive at this point, but as your business starts to grow, things are going to get hectic very quickly. Get organized now and you'll save yourself a lot of time and aggravation and maybe even some money in the future.

Now it's time to ship the records. You'll need to include what's called a "packing slip" inside each package; this is just a piece of paper that lists the name of your record label, your band and your record, the selection number, the number of records you're shipping, and the distributor's P.O. number. Repeat this information on the outside of each box as well.

Unless you happen to live close enough to the distributor's warehouse that you can drive the records there yourself, I recommend that you ship them via UPS ground service. This is the least expensive service that will allow you to track the shipment if for some reason the records don't show up where they're supposed to. It's a good idea to call the distributor after about a week to make sure the records have arrived in good shape.

Once the distributor receives your records, they will begin soliciting their accounts (i.e. convincing stores to stock the record). During this process, they may ask you to send additional one-sheets and demo copies to their sales reps. If so, do it immediately, shipping all packages UPS. Then, call the sales reps after a few days to make sure they got your packages, and introduce yourself. Remember, these people are working dozens (if not hundreds) of other records at the same time as yours—anything you can do to establish a bond with them and "put a face to your release" is going to be to your benefit, both now and in the future.

If You Don't Have "Distribution": Consignment

At this point, your distribution should be up and running. But if you weren't able to find a distributor in your first go-'round, this is the time to visit local record stores and ask them to carry your record on consignment. This means that you'll give the store a certain number of records (usually five to ten) to place on their shelves, and when the records sell through, they'll pay you a percentage of the revenue generated (usually about 60-70%). Because there's no middle-man in this situation, you'll actually make a greater profit per record under consignment than you would by going through a distributor.

Beware: record stores are notoriously lax about keeping track of their consignment stock, so it's critical that you monitor your inventory at each store, to replenish those records that have sold and get paid for them. I recommend that you check your inventory at every store that's stocking your record *at least once every two weeks.*

Chapter 10

Promoting To Radio & The Press

Thinking About Your "Record Release" Party

If you do have a distributor, it's going to take them about four to six weeks to get your record into stores, starting from the day they receive your first shipment of records. This is where timing is going to become crucial. You want to schedule the promotion to radio and the press so that it begins just as the record is starting to appear in stores. And you want to schedule your record release party so it happens about two weeks after the start of the radio/press promotion.

We're going to talk about planning the release party and other live performances in much greater depth a little later on. But for now, I just want to mention that most clubs plan their schedules about six to eight weeks in advance. And because you want to hold the release party about six to eight weeks from the time you ship the records to the distributor, the time to start lining up a venue for your record release party is now!

Step Three: Marketing

At this point, we've taken care of the first two steps of our three step sales plan: we've made a quality product and we've secured distribution for it. Now it's time for step three: making our potential customers aware that our product exists. Some people refer to this step as "marketing".

Radio Airplay

When it comes to generating awareness of your record with the music buying public, you have three main tools: radio airplay, live performance, and press coverage. Of these three tools, the most effective is radio airplay. Every time a radio station plays your song, it's as if they were playing a three minute advertisement for your record. (Actually, it's even better, since most listeners would find a three minute advertisement irritating.) And nothing convinces people to buy a new record more than hearing (and falling in love with) a new song.

Because of this, it's going to be absolutely critical for most of you to get significant radio airplay in order to sell a substantial number of records. Typically, this means you'll need to get *at least* half of the stations in your promotion to add the record. Possible exceptions to this rule include those of you involved in formats like rap and club music that don't rely heavily on radio airplay, and those of you who plan to generate most of your awareness by touring incessantly a la Blues Traveler, Phish, and of course, the Grateful Dead.

Live Performance

After radio airplay, the second most powerful awareness generator for most bands is live performance. Again, nothing sells records more effectively than the music itself. And nothing gets people (especially record people) buzzing about a band faster than a great live show.

Press Coverage

Press coverage, both in terms of record reviews and stories about your band, can also be an effective way to raise the awareness of your record among music buyers. While very few people will actually go to the store and buy a record by an unknown band based on a single review, hip music fans often go to shows based on one or more strongly positive reviews, and of course, the more times your potential buyers see your name in print, the better.

Advertising

Another way to generate awareness for your record is to buy advertising, either on radio, on TV, or in music publications. In terms of record sales, such advertisements are generally not worth their cost. Which is to say, $1,000 worth of 30-second ads on a commercial radio station probably won't sell $1,000 worth of records, nor will a $300 print ad in a national trade publication result directly in $300 worth of record sales. However, in some cases, buying ads like these might "make it a little bit easier" for that station to add your record, or that trade publication to review it.

The problem is that you never know in advance whether buying an advertisement will get you an add or a review. As a result, my advice regarding advertising is as follows: *don't buy ads either on radio or in print unless you feel it's absolutely necessary in order to "establish a relationship" with the organization in question.* In other words, you should buy an advertisement only after you've tried every other method you can think of to induce a station to add your record or a publication to review it. Don't be seduced by the idea that you can substitute ad dollars for hard work—you can't.

Mailing To Radio

Now you're ready to begin Phase One of the release (finally!) by mailing promotional packages to all the appropriate radio stations in your home base city. You want to time the mail-out so the radio stations receive the packages just as the record is starting to appear in local stores. Typically, this means you should send the packages to radio about five weeks after you send the first shipment of records to the distributor.

Each radio promo package should contain a demo copy of your CD (either punched or clipped), a T-shirt (you did make those shirts, didn't you?), a cover letter, and a trinket (read "gimmick") of some kind. The purpose of the trinket is to make opening your package a more memorable experience. The best trinkets are tied together in some way with the name of the band and/or the record and are designed to have some kind of ongoing presence in the life of the person who opens the package (hopefully the music director).

For example, one band we worked with, called Weeds Peterson, included as their trinket a miniature garden starter kit. When we called the stations to ask if they'd received the package "with the flower bulbs", every music director knew exactly what we were talking about, and several had already planted the bulbs! Based on the initial response, we decided to expand the original promotion into a contest called "Think and Grow Green with Weeds Peterson", in which prizes went to the stations who managed to grow the most bountiful gardens. (College music directors love to compete with their peers at other stations, so contests like this can be a fun and effective way to raise awareness for your release.)

Pick a trinket that will draw attention to your release, preferably one you can buy in quantities of fifty or more for a price of two dollars each or less. At this point, you probably only need to buy enough to cover all the relevant radio stations in your state. (Maybe twenty or thirty in all, depending on which state you live in.)

After you get your trinkets together, you'll need to write a cover letter addressed to "Dear Music Director". The purpose of this letter is to introduce you—the artist, not the label president—to radio station music directors and to convince them *to listen to* your record. Not necessarily to add it, just to listen to it. (You'll convince them to add it when you call them on the phone or visit them in person.)

Keep the letter brief—three paragraphs max—and keep the hype to a minimum. Unlike the cover letter you sent to the distributors, which emphasized your business plan for selling lots of records, your letter to the music directors should highlight the special qualities of the music and the band that will attract listeners for the station. If you've ever gotten an outrageous review (from virtually any publication), this might be a good place to include it. (What music director could resist listening to a record that was described as "what happens when Willie Nelson's tour bus runs over the Jackson Five"?) Also, mention any local shows you've got scheduled, and invite them to attend.

Once you get the materials together, assemble the packages and ship them Priority Mail to all the college and community stations in your home base city, as well as any commercial stations that play music in your format. As I mentioned above, you want to time the mail-out so the radio stations receive the packages just as the record is starting to appear in local stores, which generally means you should send the radio packages about five weeks after you send your first shipment to the distributor.

...And The Press

The day after you send the packages to the radio stations, make up some more packages, this time for local music writers and editors. These packages should be identical to the ones you sent to the radio stations, except they should include press kits (with photos) in addition to all the other elements.

If for some reason, you haven't had the time to assemble a press kit, it's probably okay to just send a bio along with a photo. (As I mentioned earlier, most press kits get tossed as soon as the package is opened anyway.) Obviously, you'll need to edit the cover letter so it applies to press people rather than radio people. Once you've made the changes, assemble the packages and send them to your press contacts via Priority Mail.

Back To The Fax

The day after you send the packages to the press (i.e., two days after you send them to radio) you should send a fax to both the press and the radio folks to let them know that your record will soon be arriving in the mail. This fax should be only one or two sentences, and should preferably be tied-in with the theme of your record (or your gimmick). For example, if you chose to call your record "Cheese", you could send a fax featuring a block of swiss with the heading: "Something cheesy is on its way to your mailbox."

The purpose of this fax is just to grab the attention of the reader so that when your package arrives a few days later, they'll see it and say to themselves, "Oh, *that* was what they were talking about!" Again: you're trying to make the experience of seeing and opening your package as memorable as possible (and not in a bad way).

Making Call Sheets

After you send the faxes, it's time to make your call sheets. Call sheets are tables in which you keep track of where you are in the promotion process. I recommend that you make one table for the press calls and another for the radio calls. You can make these tables in either a word processor or a spread sheet program. (Either one will do just fine.)

On the Press Call Sheet: the rows of the table will consist of the different publications to which you are promoting the record. The columns (from left to right) will consist of the Publication Name, Contact Name, Phone Number, Fax Number, Best Time(s) To Call, Status, and Notes. You'll use the "Status" column to record where you are in the promotion process—in the case of the press call sheet, you'll track information like: have they gotten the record, have they listened to it, are they going to review it, has it already been reviewed, did you get a copy of the review, did you fax it to retailers, etc.

The Radio Call Sheet will be identical to the Press Call Sheet, except that the rows will consist of the different radio stations to which you're promoting the record, and the Status column will be used to track whether they've added the record, how many times it's being played each week (also known as "spins per week"), whether you've sent extra copies, called about scheduling an interview or live performance, etc.

I know it's a pain in the neck to set up these tables, especially if you're not very familiar with your spread sheet or word processor program, but it's something you've absolutely got to do in order to stay on top of your promotion. You're going to be making a lot of calls and talking to a lot of people in the coming months, and there's no way you're going to be able to keep track of who's doing what with your record if you don't write it all down in one well-organized place.

Being the hyper-organized types we are, we've taken this process even one-stop further and created folders on our computer called "Press Call Sheets" and "Radio Call Sheets" in which we store the call sheets from our past record promotions. This allows us to maintain a record of every person who has ever reviewed or added our records—information that comes in very handy when planning new releases.

To The Phones

About three days after you send the faxes (about four to five days after you send the press packages), it's time to start calling the press people to see if they got your package. You want to start calling the press people before the radio people because, in general, press people tend to decide more quickly about what they're going to do with a particular record (i.e., whether they're going to review it).

When you call, ask to speak to the music editor or writer to whom you sent the package. If they aren't available, ask to leave a message. If they offer you the option of leaving a voice mail message, do so, and leave a brief but detailed message that goes something like this:

> "Hi Mary (always refer to them by their first name), my name is David Thomas (always use your full name) from Blind Alley Records. I'm just calling to make sure you got your copy of the self-titled release by the Seeing Eye Guys—you might remember it was the one that came with a pair of dark sunglasses. If you got it, I hope you can give it a listen sometime this week. If not, please give me a call at (418) 322-0000 and I'll send you another copy ASAP. Thanks."

If you have to leave a message with a human being instead, just leave your name and the name of your label, along with a note that you'll try back later that day. If you aren't able to reach someone after calling two or three times, ask the person taking the message when you might be able to catch them. If you can't reach them at the suggested time, send another fax, this time asking the person to call you. If they don't respond to your fax, send them another whole package and start all over. If you still haven't been able to reach them after three or four weeks, two packages, six calls, and three faxes, you might consider purchasing an advertisement as a way of establishing a relationship with the publication. But remember, purchasing an advertisement in no way guarantees that you'll get a review.

If/When You Get Them On The Phone...

If/once you manage to get the editor/writer on the phone, ask her if she's gotten the package. If she hasn't, tell her you'll send another one Priority Mail, and she should expect it in two or three days.

If she has gotten it, ask her if she's had a chance to listen to it yet. (If it's only been a few days since she got it, odds are she hasn't.) She may say she's given it to a reviewer for a write-up. If so, thank her and ask how long it will take for the review to appear. Make a note of this information in the Status and Notes columns on your call sheet. When the review appears, either get yourself a copy or call the editor (or her secretary) and ask if she can send you a "tear sheet" containing the review. (You may have to ask several times before they actually send it to you.)

If, on the other hand, she says she's received your package but hasn't had a chance to listen to it, tell her your "story": i.e., explain that you're a local label, devoted to local music, trying to establish a presence in the area; this is your first release, and you'd really appreciate it if she could help you out with a review, which would make it easier for the radio stations to add it…. Finish by asking: "Can you listen to it sometime this week?" If she says yes, say: "Great, when would be a good time for me to check back in with you to see how you liked it?" This lets her know you're going to be persistent (but pleasant!) and it provides you with a little more authority the next time you call. ("Mary asked that I call her at this time…") If she says she won't be able to get to it, be nice, but ask why. If she says she'll "try" to get to it, but won't make any promises, tell her you really hope she'll be able to get to it, and ask her when you should call next.

Call back the next week at the appointed time and begin by saying: "Hi Mary, it's Dave calling back from Blind Alley—just checking in to see if you've had a chance to listen to that record by the Seeing Eye Guys that we discussed last week..." If she says yes, ask her what she thinks about a review. If she says she hasn't listened to it yet, don't say anything. Just let her squirm. If you've done your job well, she'll remember that she was supposed to listen to it this week (even if she didn't promise). Leave it up to her to tell you why she didn't get to it, and then explain to her briefly why you think this is an album her readers would benefit from hearing about. (Remember an editor's job is to inform and entertain her readers.) Finish by asking: "Do you think you'll be able to get to it this week?"

Remember The Three Ps

Unfortunately, there's no magic formula for getting your records listened to. Every person and every situation are different. And while you won't be able to get everyone to take your phone calls, you'll get through to an awful lot of people if you're quick on your feet, and remember the three Ps: be persistent, pleasant, and professional. Remember that editors and music directors are people just like you, and just like you, they have a job to do. If you show respect for them and their work, they'll usually show respect for you and yours.

How College Radio Works

We're just about ready to starting calling the college radio stations. But before we do that, this would probably be a good time to review how these stations work.

Most college radio stations "employ" a music director, a program director or station manager, and anywhere from twenty to thirty DJs. While they typically play music from a variety of formats, most college stations specialize in a single "primary" format, which is usually some form of "college rock", ranging from AAA to AOR to Modern Rock.

If the music director thinks a particular new release will be of interest to his audience, he'll put this record into something called the "add" or "new release" bin. The DJs at the station are then free to play whatever music they choose on their shows, with the exception that they must play a certain number of songs (usually three to five) from the "add" bin each hour.

The number of times a particular record gets played each week is determined by how much the DJs at the station like the record and by the audience response to the record. Every week, the music director (or his assistant) tallies the total number of times each record in the "primary format" was played and calculates something called the weekly "chart".

The chart is a list of the 30-35 songs that received the most airplay on the station over the course of the past week. If the station is a "reporter", it means that every week they report their chart information to one or more of the national trade publications, who use the information to compile their national charts of radio airplay. If the station also plays music in "specialty" formats like rap, jazz, worldbeat, and dance music, they may (or may not) keep separate additional charts for these formats, and report them to trades as well.

The take-home message is this: *in order to get significant airplay at college radio, you first have to convince the music director to place your record into the "add" bin, and then you have to convince the individual DJs to play it with increasing frequency.*

Got it? Good. But before we leave this section, there's one more thing you need to know about college radio, and that applies to college stations on the West Coast. While stations in the Midwest, South, and East tend to play music that's fairly similar to the stuff you might hear on commercial radio, college stations in the West seem to delight in playing music that no one else will play. As a result, it tends to be harder for bands that play more "accessible" music to get airplay on college stations in the West than in other regions of the country. (No one said this was going to be easy.)

Calling Radio

You want to make your initial calls to radio the day after you start calling the press people. (Basically, the two promotions will overlap, but we find it helpful to start on separate days as a way to divide the labor.) Calling radio is very similar to calling the press. Basically, you're trying to get the music director (or in some cases, a particular DJ) on the phone to ask him if he got your package and listened to it, and whether he's planning to add it. If you can't get the music director on the phone, you'll need to use the same strategies of leaving messages and sending faxes and additional packages.

For the initial promotion, which is local, see if you can set up some face-to-face meetings with music directors *in lieu* of sending packages in the mail. Meeting face-to-face is always preferable to sending a package in the mail, because it provides you with at least five to ten minutes of the music director's undivided attention (maybe more, in the case of a smaller station). Use this time to introduce yourself, explain briefly who you are and what you're trying to do, and then play the two or three tracks you think are most likely to impress.

After you play the tracks, ask the music director what he thinks. If he likes it, ask him if he'll add it. If he says yes, thank him and ask if he'd be willing to distribute some additional copies to DJs at the station. If he says yes (and he probably will), give him three or four more copies of the record.

Why You Should Provide Additional Copies

Why give the station additional copies of the record? After all, they only need one to play on the air, don't they? Yes. But remember, once the music director places your record in the "add" bin, its fate will be determined by the DJs themselves. If they've never heard your record (or at least heard *of* it) they're probably not going to play it on their show. But if you provide them with additional copies, the DJs will have the opportunity to take your record home with them, where they can play it, fall in love with it, and decide that they simply must share it with their listeners. The more they play it, the more the audience will request it. Get the picture?

That's why *any time your record gets added at a college radio station, you should immediately send three or four more copies to the music director of that station, along with a note requesting that he distribute them to the DJs who would most likely enjoy your music.* But be sure the copies you send are all either punched or clipped as "demos", or they're likely to end up in used record stores. (Actually, some of them will undoubtedly end up in used record stores anyway... just another cost of doing business.)

Following Up

When you meet with a music director face-to-face, you should be able to get an answer on-the-spot as to whether he'll add your record. If you're conducting the entire promotion over the phone, you might need to call several times before you can get a straight yes (add) or no ("pass"). If a particular MD refuses to give you a straight answer even after several conversations, don't be afraid to say something like: "If you really have no intention of adding the record, I'd appreciate it if you could tell me now." While rejection is never fun, it's always better to know up front than to waste your time talking to someone who has no intention of adding your record. Regardless of the outcome, be sure to record on your call sheet how your record is doing at every station in your promotion.

In my experience, the most common mistake indie bands make in promoting their own records is that they fail to follow-up with music directors after their record has been added. It is absolutely crucial that you call each of the stations that have added your record *every week for at least eight weeks* to find out how the record is doing. If the record is climbing the charts, that's great! (And that's information you can use to get reviews, adds at other stations, and bookings in clubs.)

If the audience response to your record is flat (and even if it isn't), ask the music director what you might be able to do to improve it. This might be a good time to call your friends and fans and anyone else you've ever met and ask them to call the station to request your record. This would also be a good time to find out whether the station has a local music show featuring performances by local bands. (Most college stations do.) If they do, get the name of the DJ for this show, and find out when the show airs. Call the DJ during the show, introduce yourself, explain that the station just added your new record, and tell her you'd like to play live on her show.

If the station lacks the ability to broadcast live performances, maybe you could tape a show at a local club or recording studio, or even in your own practice space. Or maybe you could just do an interview over the phone. Many college stations sponsor local music shows in area clubs. Ask about that as well.

Nothing Succeeds Like Success

In the last section, I mentioned that you can use postive audience feedback at radio to help convince music editors to review your record. This tactic of using success in one area of your promotion to generate successes in others is called "cross promoting", and it is absolutely *the* key to building the buzz that will make your record release and your career a success.

There's no doubt about it—it's a thrill to see your record reviewed in the local newspaper (especially if it's a good review) or to hear it played on a local college station. You've spent a lot of time, energy, and money giving life to your musical vision, and you *should* feel a great sense of accomplishment in seeing your record get the exposure it deserves.

But remember, the goal of your record release is to sell as many records and generate as much excitement about your group as possible. To do that, you can't afford to just sit back and bask in the glow of your accomplishments. To really grow your career, you've got to pounce on your accomplishments and use them to create even greater ones.

For example, let's say you get your record added at your local college radio station. Great. As I suggested earlier, you can use this victory to get your foot in the door with the DJ of the local music show and schedule an on-air performance. Once you schedule the performance, you can then fax and mail press releases to local music writers and record retailers. Maybe your local newspaper will run a little feature story on you and your new record label, mentioning that you'll be playing live on the air in the coming week. Then you can set up a meeting with the manager of your local record store to see if you can schedule an in-store performance the day after the radio broadcast. And if things go well there, you can use the publicity generated by the event to get an opening slot at a nearby club.

If nothing else, you can definitely use the positive response at the first radio station in your conversations with music directors from other stations: "Yeah, Dave, the listeners at KXXX really love the second track. It was just added last week, and they've already gotten twenty phone calls and moved the record up to ten spins a week... now we're setting up an on-air performance, and we've been promised a feature story in the *Daily Gazette*."

The Upward Spiral

This is how you do it, moving back and forth between radio, the press, live performances, and miscellaneous other buzz-building activities, ping-pong-ing your way up the ladder of success. Every time you succeed, your story gets a little bit more impressive; the more impressive your story becomes, the more opportunities you'll have to add to it.

The beautiful (and maddening) thing about promoting records is that you never know which events are going to be the ones that really open doors for you until you try them. You may schedule a show opening up for a major label touring band only to have the show cancelled at the last minute, and then find out that the owner of the hardware store whose grand opening you played last week is best friends with the assistant editor of *Spin*.

And because you never know which opportunities are going to be the ones that really move your career forward, you have to dedicate yourself to the idea that *you are going to chase down every lead, no matter how meaningless it may seem at the time, and do everything you possibly can to expose your music to the public*. Because the fact is: you never know who's going to be out there listening.

How Commercial Radio Works

Before we leave this chapter, I want to say a few words about promoting your record to commercial radio. As I mentioned earlier, the folks at commercial radio tend to be very conservative about which records they play. It's very rare for a commercial station to "take a chance" on a new band unless either the band has already done very well at similar stations or the band's label has provided an inducement for the station to play the record, usually in the form of co-op advertising.

Because neither of these things will be true for your band, at least in the initial stages of your release, you're going to find it extremely difficult to get the commercial stations in your area to play your record on anything other than a local music show (if they even have one).

But don't let that deter you from sending your record to commercial stations in your format. *You should definitely send it to them*, for several reasons. For one thing, there are exceptions to every rule, and as I just got finished saying, you never know what's going to happen in any particular situation until you give it a try. While you probably won't be able to get the music director to add your record, you might be able to find an individual DJ who likes it enough to play it during an evening or weekend show. That will introduce your music to tens of thousands of people who have never heard it before, and it will allow you to include the commercial station on your list of "stations playing the record".

Also, even though a commercial station might not add your record at this stage, it's important to begin developing your relationship with them now so they can share in the "story" of your record as it builds over the course of the release. Think of it this way: what's more exciting—to see the last two minutes of a football game you've been watching all day, or to walk into a room just before the final play and have to have someone explain to you what's been happening the entire game? Establish your relationships now so the folks at the big stations will already be familiar with you if and when you're ready for them.

A Word Of Advice About Indie Promoters

Many musicians planning their first release find the entire subject of radio promotion so intimidating that, rather than even try to run the promotion themselves, they decide to hire an independent promotion company. On the surface of it, hiring an indie promoter sounds like a great idea: for a few hundred dollars a week, you get to have a professional promoter (complete with all of his/her "relationships") work your record to hundreds of stations across the country. If things go well, you could be added on a hundred stations or more, maybe even chart in one of the trades, and bring yourself to the attention of A&R reps near and far.

However, having worked as an independent promoter myself, I can tell you that there are several problems with this plan. First, in order to maximize their income, professional indie promoters usually work anywhere from five to ten records at a time. Because of this, it's unlikely that your record will get the kind of personal attention it needs to succeed, let alone the kind of attention you would give it were you to make the calls yourself.

Another problem with using an indie promoter is the design of the promotional campaign itself. Rather than start the promotion locally and build it outward slowly over time as I suggest, most indie promoters will want to send your record to several hundred stations *at the same time*, usually with little or no regard for whether those stations have significant listening audiences, or even whether they're appropriate for your style of music. Many indie promotional campaigns include high school stations, cable-current stations, and college stations with virtually no listeners. Getting airplay on these stations isn't going to sell records or provide meaningful exposure, and it certainly isn't going to impress anyone at a major label.

And even if you were to get added on a hundred "real" stations, at this point you don't have anywhere near the money or the clout you'd need to get your records stocked in stores near all those stations, nor could you possibly hope to go play shows at most of them while they're still spinning your record.

Now let's say you're a major label A&R rep and you're considering signing a new group. The very first thing you're probably going to want to do after signing them is to take their most recent release, repackage it, and re-release it with a solid national push. (Prominent examples of bands that have benefitted from this strategy include Everclear, Better Than Ezra, Jennifer Trynin, and Emmet Swimming.) However, if the record has already been sent to all the college stations you would have included in the first round of your promotion, you've got a problem. Obviously, any station that has already played the record for a few weeks or months and then "retired" it to the "recurrent" bin isn't going to want to add it again just because it was re-released by a major label. And any station that passed on the record the first time because the band didn't have distribution and/or wasn't touring probably won't even give the record a second listen. Because of this, you're going to have a very difficult time generating the kind of momentum you need at college radio in order to get the record played at commercial stations.

So, while the thought of spending a few thousand dollars to get your record played on a hundred or more stations nationwide sounds attractive, the fact is that *without sufficient distribution and tour support, promoting your record to hundreds of stations simultaneously is more likely to damage your career (maybe irreparably) than it is to help.*

My advice is: if you can find an independent promoter who will give your record the attention it needs in order to thrive, and who will promote it to a manageable number of stations initially and then grow with you over time, it might be worth your investment. Otherwise, you're better off promoting your record yourself.

Chapter 11

Playing Live

Yes, You Need To!

Of all the things you can do to generate excitement about your band and your record, there's nothing more powerful than playing live shows. I'm often approached by people who want to know whether they really need to play live in order become successful musicians. The answer is: *yes!* You must play live, you must do it often, and you must do it very, very well.

While booking shows can be very frustrating, and promoting them can be a lot of work (if done correctly), the benefits of playing live far outweigh the disadvantages. For one thing, it's a blast. I can't think of a better way to reduce the stress induced by countless rejections and unreturned phone calls than to get up on a stage and sing your heart out for an hour or three.

For another thing, playing live puts you in touch with your audience (and the audiences of others) in a way that nothing else can. When you play live, your fans get to experience you up close and in the flesh... they get to feel that they're an essential part of the experience. And if you put on a great show, you can make an impression on your audience that will last a lifetime.

And while your fans are getting to experience you, you'll get to experience them! In addition to the adrenalin rush brought on by the thunderous applause and adulation of your listeners, you'll get critical feedback about which songs generate the most positive response. This is information you can use to select which songs you'll push at radio, and even to help convince music directors to add them.

Another great thing about playing live is that it gives you something to promote. This is particularly true of your record release party. A show is an event. It's a place where people can go to see you play, bring their friends, shmooze with other industry types, dance, and generally just hang out. It's one thing to send someone a record and ask them to add it or review it. It's quite another to give them a record and then invite them to a show you're playing the next weekend. *You're much more likely to get radio airplay and write-ups in the press, both locally and far from home, if you gig regularly.*

Shows are also a great place to make money. Selling T-shirts and records at your shows will bring in some much needed cash and create another source of exposure for your band and your record. And as your popularity grows and you start to draw larger crowds, you might even start to make some money at the door.

If all that isn't enough to get you out there playing, remember: musicians aren't the only ones who know the power of live shows to generate excitement and sell records—the people who run record labels know it too. Nothing will catch the attention of an A&R rep faster than a band that draws 500 people every time they play.

Record people not only want to see that you *can* play live; they want to see that you *do* play live, that you do it often (at least once a week), and that you draw big crowds (averaging at least 150 people).

How To Get Gigs

Getting gigs is very similar to getting radio airplay. First, you make a list of the venues you want to play. Then you mail or hand deliver promo packages. And then you start calling.

Hopefully you've already made a list of all the clubs and other venues in your area that you might want to play. If you're not sure where you should play, call local radio stations in your format and ask them where their listeners go to see shows.

Before you send the packages, call the clubs on your list to find out when they take booking calls, and whether you should send your demo on CD or cassette. (Believe it or not, many club bookers, or "talent buyers" as they sometimes like to be called, don't have CD players.) If they ask for a cassette and your release is CD only, dub your four best songs onto a tape (best song first!) and label the tape with your band's name and phone number. Even if they ask for a cassette, it's probably a good idea to include a copy of your CD as well, which will lend extra credibility to the entire package.

Along with the tape or CD, you should include a brief cover letter (three paragraphs max) to introduce yourself and your band, tell your story (highlighting any radio airplay or press coverage you've received or been promised), and ask for a gig. It's always a good idea to mention that you have a "large and growing following" (or at least a "growing following") and to suggest a few ways that you plan to promote the gig (on-air or in-store performances, handing out flyers in competing clubs, playing on street corners, etc.) Finish by mentioning that you'll call the next week at the suggested time to discuss scheduling.

In addition to the CD/tape and the cover letter, include the three best write-ups you've gotten to date (as long as they're less than two years-old), and a trinket. Unless you can personally hand your package to the talent buyer, send it Priority Mail. Then call (or send a fax if the club has one) to let her know the package is coming and ask her to listen to it as soon as possible.

Calling (...And Calling)

The people who book clubs are notoriously overworked, underpaid, and deluged with tapes. It's not unusual for a booker at a good-sized club in a major city to receive as many as fifty or even one hundred tapes every week. Most bookers tell us they want to be fair to the bands that submit demos, but they just don't have the time to listen to and judge all the tapes they get. So, while some clubs will let you play on a weeknight based only on your demo tape, others won't even listen to your tape unless they've seen your name a few times in the local press (concert listings, record reviews, etc.) Given this, your strategy should be to start in the clubs that will book you now, and then do everything you can to generate the buzz that's going to get you a foot in the door at the larger clubs.

Shmooze With Other Musicians

There are several things you can do to increase your chances of getting quality gigs. The first is to meet and "hang" with as many up-and-coming musicians as you can. Keep yourself well informed about which bands play where and when. If there are bands that gig regularly at a club you'd like to play, introduce yourself to them and give them a copy of your CD. Then call back a few days later to see how they liked it, and ask them if you can open for them sometime. If you have a good following at a particular club, you might offer to suggest them as an opening band to the talent buyer at that club. At the very least, you should be familiar enough with your "scene" that you're able to suggest to bookers which bands you'd like to play with.

Open For Major Label Bands

Another way to get good gigs is to contact the managers and agents of major label bands that will soon be touring in your area, and tell them you'd like to open for their group when they come to town. Keep your eyes and ears peeled to local concert listings to find out which bands will be coming to town as far in advance as possible. Then send promo packages (Priority Mail) to their manager, their agent, and maybe even their A&R rep telling them you'd like to open for them. You want to portray yourself as the hottest local band on the scene, generating a big buzz with your new CD, and able to draw a large crowd for their show. In addition to contacting the band's "people", be sure to suggest yourself as an opening act to the talent buyer for the club as well. In some cases, it will be the talent buyer who makes the decision to book you as the opening act, with the "permission" of the headliner's agent or manager.

Getting opening slots in this way is not easy. Major label managers and agents are very busy people, and they can be very difficult to contact by phone. But if you're persistent, you may just find yourself playing for a thousand people in the biggest club in town.

Fax Regular Updates

Finally, do everything you can to keep your name in the minds of club bookers. The best way to do this is by faxing. Every time your record gets added or makes a big jump in the charts at a station in your area, send a brief press release to the clubs. Every time you get a review, fax a copy. If you schedule an on-air performance or interview, fax an announcement. Basically, you should strive to send one fax a week (max) that contains at least one new piece of significant information. If nothing else, the bookers will see that you're on the ball (and if you're lucky, they might even remember your name).

In short, getting gigs is a demanding (and sometimes a demeaning) job. You can expect people to blow you off, lose your tape, break promises, and generally treat you badly. But don't let it get you down, and don't take it personally. If someone loses your tape, send another, and another... FedEx if necessary. If they don't remember promising you a gig the previous week, remind them (nicely!). But above all, keep calling and keep faxing. With patience and perserverance, you will succeed.

Promoting Your Shows

Maybe the world would be a better place if people flocked to clubs every night to see bands they had never heard of. But the reality is that people don't go to see bands they've never heard of, and they never will. So if you want people to come see you, you better become a band they've heard of (or at least *open* for a band they've heard of). And the way to do that is by promoting your shows.

For starters, try to make sure that the cover charge is low (under $5 on weekends, $3 on weeknights). If you're playing with other bands, find out who they are and call them as far in advance as possible. Ask them what they're doing to promote the show, share your ideas, and see if they want to work together. (This is also a great way to meet new people and extend your "network".)

You've probably figured out that unless you already have a loyal following flyers won't do much to bring people to your shows. But they're still great for increasing name recognition, so ask local businesses if they'll let you put a flyer in their window. And don't limit yourself to music and record stores! Try to get flyers into any store that draws a lot of foot traffic: restaurants, cafes, delis, clothing stores, movie theatres, etc. You might want to make some of your flyers double-sided so they can be seen from both sides of a window.

The Personal Touch—Handbills

About two weeks before the show, print up 2,000 handbills on colorful paper (four per sheet of 8.5" x 11"). that contain an announcement for the show, along with a message that says, "Bring this handbill to the show and you'll receive a copy of the new CD by [your band name here] absolutely free!" Distribute these handbills anywhere and everywhere you can think of: clubs, restaurants, and movie theatres, street corners, shopping malls and parks, etc. Don't worry that you'll be overwhelmed by people wanting free CDs. You won't be, and even if you were, it would probably be the best that had ever happened to your career. The idea is to make people aware that you exist, that you've just released a new record, and that you'll soon be playing nearby.

Play On Street Corners

Try to spend several afternoons or evenings a month promoting your shows by playing on high-traffic street corners for passers-by. (If your music is a little more hard core, you might consider doing an "unplugged" version or just playing your CD on a boom box while you talk up your show.) Move around to different neighborhoods, distributing handbills as you go. Have a friend take your picture and then send it to local papers with an announcement of your gig.

Promote Your Shows On Radio, In Record Stores

Visit the radio stations on your list and invite the music director and the DJs (and anyone else you can find) to the show. If they're playing your record already, ask them to announce the gig on the air. If there's going to be a cover charge for the gig, ask the club if you can offer DJs free tickets to use as give-aways. And as we discussed ealier, try to schedule an on-air performance or interview for a few days before a big gig.

Visit your local record stores, especially the ones that are stocking your record, and ask them to put up flyers in the window. (Don't show them the handbills—they won't be happy to see you giving away free CDs to all your fans!) Some retailers will even let you put a gig announcement right above the rack where your CD is displayed. Be sure to tell all the people behind the counter and especially the store manager about the gig, and offer to include them on the "free" list. (If it looks like you're going to exceed the number of people on your free list, ask the club for more freebies, and/or ask if you can buy some advance tickets to the show and then give those away instead.)

Send Postcards

Of course, you should also send postcards announcing the gig to everyone on your mailing list, including the folks at radio, retail, and the press, your distributor, booking agencies, other clubs, and your fans. If you'd like to save money by including several gigs on one postcard, that's fine. (In fact, when you're trying to impress industry people, the more gigs you have on a card the better.)

The More Unusual The Better

Those are some of the standard things you can and should do to promote your performances. But don't stop there. Use your creativity to come up with new and exciting ways of promoting yourself—and remember, the more "unconventional" your promotions are, the more exposure they're likely to generate.

For example, you might run a contest at a local high school where the winning contestants get to sing back-up on a song during an all-ages show. Hold auditions at a school assembly and let the students pick the winners. This will dramatically increase the awareness of your band among the students at the school, and will encourage more of them to attend your show.

If you've got a big show coming up, you might create a special "commemorative single" on vinyl or cassette that you can give away (or sell) at the show. This can be particularly effective as a way to renew interest in your band after your record has been out for six or nine months. If you're playing with another band, you might split your costs by creating a "double A-side" single featuring one song from each band: make 500 copies, give away 100 at the show, and sell the other 400 for $3 each. (You might even make a profit.)

Schedule free performances in hospitals, senior citizen communities, and the local boys/girls club. Call up local charities and offer your services for their next fundraising event. Or even better, organize your own event and donate the proceeds to charity. And be sure to send announcements in advance and press releases afterward to everyone on your press list.

Don't like any of these ideas? Fine. Come up with some of your own. And remember, there are no rules about what you can and can't do. (Laws maybe, but no rules.) But whatever you do, don't sit around waiting for someone to come and build a following for you, 'cause it ain't gonna happen. If you want attention, you're going to have to go out there and get it yourself. (And if you don't want attention, you're in the wrong business.)

Making The Most Of Your Live Performances

Of course, drawing a big crowd isn't going to do you any good if you don't put on a great show for them. (In fact, it will probably do you more harm than if you hadn't played at all!) So here are a few suggestions as to how you can make the most out of your live performances.

Be Engaging

You don't necessarily have to have the world's strongest voice or slickest guitar technique to be a great performer. What you have to have is the ability to entertain your audience, to move them, to engage them in what you're doing. Maybe it's the way you sing, maybe it's the way you move, maybe it's the way you look or even the stories you tell between songs. But if you're going to have a career in this business, you've got to be able to grab your audience and hold them.

If you don't have this ability already (don't feel bad, most people don't), there are several things you can do to develop it. The first is to just get out there and play as much as possible. The more you play, the more comfortable you'll be on stage. The more comfortable you are, the more engaging you'll be.

The second thing you can do is watch other performers you find engaging and figure out what it is that makes them so. Is it the way they dress, the way they move, their facial expressions? Try to find artists who perform the way you would if you could really be yourself on stage, and then emulate them.

Videotape your performances and study them. At which points in the show is the crowd most engaged, and why? At which points did the crowd's attention wane? Are there particular songs that work better or worse than others? (If so, consider altering or eliminating the weaker songs from the set.) Is there anything that's distracting about your appearance? Does your bass player make eye contact with the crowd, or do she stare at her shoes? Is your clothing appropriate for your style of music and does it coordinate well as a group? Does the music sound well-rehearsed? Are the harmonies in tune, etc.?

In my experience, *the three things that most impress audiences of live music are well-sung harmonies, a great horn section, and a strong visual presentation.*

In short, you need to do everything you possibly can to fine-tune the mechanics of your show and develop confidence as a performer. Be honest with yourself, but be gentle.

Mailing Lists & Merchandise

In addition to becoming a great performer, there are some logistics you'll need to take care of. For one thing, you need to make up some "mailing list" cards; these are post cards your fans will fill out in order to join your mailing list. (We find post cards preferable to a single "sign-up sheet" or notebook because, unlike the sign-up sheet, the cards can be distributed to many people at once.) Each card should have blanks for the person's name, address, and email address. (Sending gig announcements by email is faster, cheaper, and far less work than sending them through postal "snail" mail.)

Before each gig, set up a small table near the front door where you can sell CDs and T-shirts and sign people up on your mailing list. During your set, be sure to mention at least twice who you are and the fact that you have CDs and T-shirts available for sale. (It's not a bad idea for one or more band members to wear the shirt on stage.) Depending on your style of music and the average disposable income of your audience members, you should charge between $5-10 for the CD and another $5-10 for the T-shirt. Remember, you want to make *some* money, but you also want to get your music and your name out into the community as quickly as possible.

In fact, when you're just starting out, you should consider giving away your CD free to anyone who signs up on your mailing list. This is a bit costly and you're probably depriving yourself of a few would-have-been sales, but it's a great way to make an impression on your audience, get your music out there, and build up your mailing list in a hurry. (This works especially well if you're opening for a more established band and most of the people in the crowd are not yet familiar with you.)

Regardless of whether you give away CDs, you should announce near the end of your set that some people will be coming through the crowd with mailing list cards and pens. (Then have a few friends do just that.) Ask the crowd to fill out the cards. If you're going with the CD giveaway offer, instruct the crowd that they can "redeem" their cards for CDs at the merchandise table.

It's always a good idea to toss free stickers, candy, or other trinkets to the crowd from the stage, especially if the majority of your fans are college age or younger.

When the set is over—and this is crucial!—all the members of the band (or at *least* the lead singer) should come down off the *front* of the stage and thank each and every person in the crowd for listening and encourage them to sign up on the mailing list. I know this is a very hard thing to do. When you've just poured your heart out on stage, the last thing you want to do is make small talk with a bunch of people you've never met. But the fact is, *there is a critical window of about five minutes after a set in which audience members are very receptive to experiences that will shape their impression of what they just saw and heard.* This is the time for you to meet them and thank them for coming. If it's obvious they came for one of the other bands, then thank them for listening, or dancing, or whatever. But make sure you express your appreciation for their support and tell them you're looking forward to seeing them at future shows. This kind of shmoozing may not come naturally to you at first, but it's unquestionably one of the most effective things you can do to build your following. And you never know, one of the people you greet may very well be a (very impressed) major label executive.

After the show, send a follow-up mailer to all the people who just signed up on your mailing list. This should be a simple post card that thanks them for signing up and alerts them to future up-coming gigs. If you gave away CDs to everyone who signed up at your last show, you might also include a message that says "And we hope you're enjoying our new CD... [your CD name here]!" This will serve two purposes. First it will remind to listen to the CD (if they haven't already), and second, it will remind them that they've already received something from you without having to pay for it. (This makes them feel like they're a special part of your family, and will encourage them to come to another show.)

If the show was particularly successful, you might want to send a press release, along with a few black-and-white photographs if you have them, to your local music publications. If nothing else, this will let them know that your show went well, and that you're on the ball. If you're lucky, you might get a brief mention, and/or the paper might be more disposed to send a reporter to review your next show.

Last but not least, remember to follow-up with the club, either by mail or (preferably) by phone. Thank them for letting you play at their venue, remind them what a great success the entire evening was (you might mention how many people signed up on your mailing list and/or how many of your friends commented on the quality of the sound, etc.), and suggest that you'd like to play again as soon as possible. In some cases, it might be appropriate for you to try to schedule a series of regular appearances (either weekly or monthly) at the club. If this is a possibility—go for it! Regular appearances are a great way to build fan support and establish yourself as part of a local scene.

Your CD Release Party

For those of you who have never heard this term before, a "CD release party" is simply a party that you host to celebrate the release of your new CD. The idea is to create an "event" (i.e., worthy of press coverage) at which you can perform your new material for friends and fans as well as key contacts from radio, retail, and the press.

Ideally, you want to have your CD release party about two to three weeks after the beginning of your Phase One radio promotion. Hopefully by this time you've managed to get at least a few music directors to add your record and a few music writers to review it. As I mentioned earlier, many venues schedule their bookings six to eight weeks in advance (or even earlier), so you'll need to start lining up the venue for your release party right after you set up your account with the distributor.

Booking The Event

Try to book your CD party into a venue that's either impressive or unusual (or both), but still appropriate for the size of your fanbase: clubs are the most common choice, but don't overlook "alternative" venues like museums, schools, or even warehouses. If you'd like to book your party into a particular club but don't feel your following is large enough to justify it, consider holding the party on a friday or saturday *evening* (i.e., before 9:00 p.m.). Many clubs that would charge you $1,000 to use their room from 10:00 to midnight on a Friday will let you use it for free from 7:00-9:00.

If a club is hesitant about letting you use their room for your

party, explain to them that you are planning to draw at least fifty people (or more, if it's true), that you'll be catering the event with hors
d'oevres, etc., and that you'll want to buy some champagne from
them in order to toast your new release. You might also mention how
you plan to promote the show (radio interviews, press advertisements, personal invitations, etc.) Hopefully, they'll let you have the
use of their room "free of charge". If they do try charge you for the
room, think about holding your party elsewhere. But whatever you
do, don't pay more than $100 or so to rent a room for your CD
release party—it's just not worth it.

Invitation Only

Once you get the room lined up, it's time to make your invitations. The idea here is to make something that looks better than a
postcard without spending a lot of money. You should be able to
make a suitable invitation on your computer (*italic* typefaces work
nicely):

> *Dear   ,*
>
> *You are cordially invited to a party at <name of venue> to
> celebrate the brand new release <name of release> by
> <name of band>. The party will be held on <date of party>
> at <time of party>. Hors d'oevres will be served as well as
> a complimentary champagne toast, after which the band will
> perform some selections from the new CD.*
>
> *The courtesy of a reply is requested: (222) 444-6666.*

Design theinvitation so that four copies will fit onto a single
8.5"x11" sheet of paper. Take this paper down to your local copy
center and use it to make 100 invitations (twenty-five sheets) on a
nice card stock. Then buy some suitable envelopes, address them,
and mail them right after you send the promo packages to the radio
stations.

Obviously, you want to send invitations to all the music directors and DJs at your local stations, as well as all the music writers and editors on your press list. You should also send invitations to your distributor reps, your contacts at retail stores, and any other music industry "movers and shakers" in your vicinity. (Most of them won't come to the show, but sending them an invitation is a classy way to let them know about your release.) If you don't mind spending a few extra dollars on postage, you might even send these "formal" invitations to your friends and fans so they understand the importance of attending the show.

Other than that, your CD release party is pretty much the same as any other gig: if you want it to be a success, you've got to get out there and promote the heck out of it, using all the techniques discussed above (and maybe a few of your own). The night of the show, make a point of greeting each and every person who walks through the door. (Remember, these are the people on your local scene who can really help your record and career.) Have one of your articulate friends make the toast to you and your new record just before your band takes the stage to play a set of six to eight songs from the new release. Be sure to have some CDs and T-shirts on-hand to use as door prizes, etc.

What To Expect

Don't be too disappointed if you have a difficult time getting the people on your VIP list to attend your release party. It's probably nothing personal, and it's certainly not an indication that your release will not go well. The fact is, most of these people have been to hundreds of release parties, and unless they're already familiar with a particular band, they're probably not going to be very excited about going to another one. And while a release party can be a useful promotional device, it's certainly not the make-or-break event many people think it is.

Try to think of your release party as a chance for you to throw a nifty little shindig for your friends and a few industry contacts. Don't spend too much money ($300 max), and above all, enjoy yourself—it's a party.

One last thing about release parties: there's no reason to limit yourself to just one. If, during the later stages of the promotion, you're expanding into a new city and you want to make a splash with the local DJs, writers, agents, etc., why not throw yourself another little party? Remember, as far as the people in that city are concerned, your CD *is* new. So why not celebrate its release? (And again, this can be a useful way of getting into a club that otherwise might not book you.)

Chapter 12

Expanding
The Promotion

Are You Making Headway?

After you've been promoting your record in your home base city for about eight to twelve weeks, it's time to assess your progress. By this point, you should be getting fairly significant airplay on at least three different stations in your area; you should have been reviewed, interviewed, or at least mentioned in at least three different local publications, and you should be drawing at least 100 people to a gig at least one out of every ten nights. If you are—great. It's time to start thinking about expanding your promotion to surrounding cities.

If You're Having Difficulty

If, however, you're having difficulty getting people to play your record and/or come to your live shows, you need to take a good hard look at what you're doing to promote yourself, and try to figure out where you're having difficulty. For example, were you able to meet with music directors, or at least get them to listen to your record? If not, you need to think about what you can do to get your foot in the door. If you were able to get them to listen to it, were you able to get them to add it? If not, what was it specifically about the record that kept them from adding it? If they did add it, what kind of response did they get? Did you take pains to ensure that the appropriate DJs got their own personal copies? Did you follow up with the station to schedule interviews and on-air performances? Did you provide them with CDs, T-shirts, and concert tickets to use as promotional give-aways?

Regarding your live performances, did you get to meet with talent buyers, or at least convince them to give your tape a serious listen? Were you able to schedule gigs? If not, did you approach other bands about opening for them? Did you promote your shows relentlessly? Did you spend at least ten nights a month either passing out flyers or playing on street corners? Do you know the names of ten different people who work behind the counter at no less than three different record stores? Did you give away free CDs at your shows to get people signed up on your mailing list? Did you come down off the front of the stage and personally introduce yourself to every single person in the crowd?

If the answer to any of these questions is "no", then you can probably be doing more to promote your record. I can hear you saying: "What do you mean we could be doing more? We're working our butts off!" And here's what I have to say in response: I know you're working your butts off—in fact, you've probably never worked so hard in your life—but the fact is, if what you're doing so far isn't working, you've only got two choices: work harder or give up. I know it's not what you want to hear, but the choice is up to you.

If, on the other hand, you've tried every trick in this book (and maybe a few tricks of your own), and you still haven't been able to get people to play your record or come to your shows, then you need to reassess your music and your market. Think about the responses you got when you asked music directors, writers, and talent buyers what they didn't like about your record. Was it the songwriting? The performance? The production? If most everyone had the same criticism, you need to give it some serious consideration. Because if everyone in your home city thinks there's a problem with the record, it's pretty likely that people in other places will too. If that's the case, you're better off ending the promotion now and refocusing your resources on making your next record (and making it better!) There's no reason to beat yourself up about it. This is not failure. It's simply artistic growth (and good business).

If, on the other hand, people tell you that they like the music, but it really doesn't fit in with what they're doing, you need to decide whether there are alternate channels available locally for you to promote your music, or whether you might be better off moving to a different home base city. Again, if you're a modern rock artist in Houston, this might be the time to consider moving to Dallas.

If your music is truly "alternative"—i.e., it doesn't sound like *anything* being played on the radio—then it's time to start getting creative and look for ways to promote your music that don't depend on radio airplay. Unfortunately, this subject is beyond the scope of this book, but I do recommend that you study other alternative performers and make an effort to contact them to discuss how they've managed to build a successful career. (Hundreds of performers have managed to build profitable and rewarding careers without ever getting to hear themselves on the radio.)

The Go-Slow Approach

Okay. We've talked a lot about what to do if your campaign isn't going quite as well as you'd hoped. But what if things are going pretty well (or even better!) after ten to twelve weeks? If this is the situation in which you find yourself… congratulations! It's time to expand your promotion from your home base city to other cities in your surrounding area. How large a surrounding area? Well, a good rule of thumb is that you should include any city that's close enough that you could (and would) drive there to play a single show and then drive home the same night. For most bands, this means you should *expand the promotion to all the cities within about 150 miles of you that have a reasonably large market for your style of music.*

Many bands make the mistake of expanding their initial promotion too broadly too quickly. They think that in order to impress A&R reps they have to get 150 stations to play their record at the same time so they can chart in *CMJ*. They also think that if a radio station doesn't add their record within three weeks of the initial release that they never will.

Neither of these things are true. For one thing, charting in *CMJ* is a lot less important than you might think. A chart position may get you a call from an A&R rep's secretary requesting a copy of your record, but it's not going to get you much else. (If you don't believe me, call up some indie bands that have charted in *CMJ* and ask them how much good it did for their careers.) And in any case, you certainly do not *need* to chart in *CMJ* to build a track record that will attract the attention of major labels.

For another thing, even if you do have the resources to promote your record to 150 stations simultaneously, you don't have the resources to effectively support a promotion this large with distribution and live performances. And if even if you did, it would *still* be a better idea to build the promotion gradually. Because no matter how well you could promote the release to 150 stations over the course of two months, it only stands to reason that you could do a better job promoting to those same stations over a span of six months. That's four extra months to tour, line up interviews, get to know DJs, expand your relationship with your distributor, etc.

And if you're worried that a station in Ohio won't add your record if it's already been "out" for four months, don't be. As far as stations outside your home region are concerned, your record hasn't been "released" until it appears in the area of their broadcast. And don't forget, a station is much more likely to add your record if other stations with similar audiences have gotten a good response with it, even if those stations are located in other states.

So don't make the mistake of expanding your promotion to quickly. You'll be more successful and have a better time if you take it slowly.

Phase Two: The Surrounding Cities

The first thing you should do in expanding your promotion is to select the cities you'll target next. As I mentioned above, you want to include any city within about 150 miles of you that has at least one reasonably large college or community station, at least one adequate venue where you can perform, *and* one reasonably large commercial station in your format. For example, if your homebase is San Francisco, you should now be expanding to San Jose, Oakland,

Berkeley, and Sacramento. If your homebase is Columbus, Ohio, you should expand to Cincinnati, Cleveland, and maybe Akron, Dayton, and Toledo.

If your homebase city is not within 150 miles of another "major market", you'll have to look farther afield. But remember that you should only include in your promotion those cities that have a market for *your style of music*.

After you've selected the cities you'll target in the next round of your promotion, go back to your *CMJ* directory or other industry information books (or talk to your distributor) and make a list of all the relevant college, community, and commercial stations in those cities. Then, call these stations to get updated address, phone, and fax information, and ask them for a list of stores (with street addresses if possible) where their listeners go to buy records.

After you've made a list of all the stores you'd like to get your record into, call the distributor and tell them you're planning to expand the promotion, and then describe which stations you'll be promoting to, and which stores you'd like to cover.

Deja Vu All Over Again

Now it's time for the Phase Two radio mail-out. In Phase One of the promotion, you had to wait four to five weeks after you mailed to the distributor before you sent the records to radio and the press. But this time, the distributor will already be up and running with the record, so you should mail the promo packages to radio stations immediately after contacting the distributor. By the time the music directors get the packages and listen to them, the record should be starting to appear in local record stores.

After you mail the records to radio, make a list of the relevant music publications in the area of the expanded promotion and mail out press packages just as you did in Phase One. This would also be a good time to get a list of all the clubs where you might want to play and send them packages as well. (By the time you get them to listen to the material, you should have something going on in the way of airplay and/or reviews.)

Then, it's back to the phones to promote your record to radio and the press, just as you did in Phase One. All the same rules apply. Remember the power of faxing and personal visits. If and when a station adds your record, send three to four extra copies immediately, and above all, *remember to follow up.* Call music directors *at least* once every two weeks to see how your record is doing, and suggest on-air interviews and performances, product giveaways, etc. If you get good audience response at a particular station, use that information to schedule a gig at a nearby club and/or record store as soon as possible.

As Your Story Grows...

It's a good idea to send weekly or bi-weekly faxes to all the music directors, writers, and talent buyers on your list to let them know how the story of your record is building. Of course, this is only a good idea if the story of your record actually *is* building. If, over the course of a week or two, you've gotten one or two new adds, you've been bumped from light to medium or heavy rotation, and gotten one or two new reviews, that's sufficient cause for sending an update. And if you've gotten encouraging sales reports from your distributor, that's *definitely* worthy of an update.

If, on the other hand, you haven't gotten any significant adds or reviews, and your record is stagnating at the stations that are playing it, you're probably better off not announcing that fact to the world.

Your goal is to constantly build the story of your release—in terms of radio airplay, press coverage, live draw, and most importantly, sales—in all the cities of your expanded promotion.

Chapter 13

Getting Paid

Expand Or Recall?

After about ten to twelve weeks of promoting to the cities around your home base, it's once again time to assess your progress and consider whether to expand to Phase Three. If, after this time, your record is getting significant airplay on at least 50% of the college and community stations on your list (and maybe one or two commercial stations as well), you're playing gigs to at least fifty people at least five times a month, and you're selling at least twenty-five records in each city of the promotion every week, you probably have enough of a story to expand the promotion to surrounding states.

If, on the other hand, less than half of the stations in your promotion are playing the record despite your best efforts, and/or record stores are starting to return your product to the distributor, it's probably time to end the promotion and "recall" the record.

If this is the situation in which you find yourself, don't despair. As I said before, deciding to end a promotion is not a sign of defeat. It simply means that you've come to the realization that you've done all you can do with this record (at least for now), and that you'll be better off saving your remaining resources for your next release. And of course, ending the promotion has one very large fringe benefit— you can finally get paid by your distributor (if you haven't gotten paid already).

Recalling Your Record

If you do decide to end your promotion, the first thing you should do is notify your distributor. Unless your record is still selling fairly well and you plan to release another record (either by your band or by another one on your label) within the next six months, you should recall the record. This simply means that you are officially asking the distributor to return all unsold merchandise from warehouses and record stores to you and pay for all sold merchandise by a certain date.

To recall your record, send a one-paragraph fax to the distributor that reads:

> I authorize the return of the record "<name of record>" by the artist "<name of artist>" from all stores in which it has been placed. All unsold product should be returned to <name of record label> no later than 120 days from today, <today's date>. Payment in full for all merchandise not returned should be made to <name of record label> no later 180 days from today.

If you're planning to close your account with the distributor (and pursue another line of work), you'll have to pay the cost of shipping the unsold and damaged records back from the distributor to you. If, however, you're planning to release more records in the future, either by your group or another, you should keep the account open, and the distributor should pay the cost of returning the records. If the distributor asks you to pay for shipping, tell them you're planning to release more records in the near future and you'd appreciate it if they would pick up the shipping costs this time around.

If all goes well, the distributor will return all the damaged and unsold records to you at their expense within 120 days of your request, and you'll receive payment in full for all the records that sold within another 60 days. If you don't receive payment from the distributor within 60 days, send another request for payment in writing (by mail and by fax). If they still don't pay, keep sending written requests for payment once every two weeks for a period of sixty more days. If they still haven't paid you by this time, send them another written notice indicating that you intend to bring suit against them. Hopefully, this will elicit some response on their part. If it doesn't, you might want to consider hiring a "collection agency" or even taking them to court (if you have access to inexpensive legal service).

Save Those Records!

Depending on how many records you pressed intially and how many you sold during the promotion, you may find that you have a substantial number of records left over after the promotion is complete and the record has been recalled. What should you do with them? Well, whatever you do, don't throw them away! Even though it may seem like no one wants them right now, demand for your first record will be renewed if your second (or even your third) release starts to generate a good buzz. It's very common for bands to re-release their first record to stores along with their second release. (Often, if a music buyer likes your second record, he'll want to stock your earlier material as well.) And at the very least, you can use copies of the first CD as giveaways at shows to get people signed up on your mailing list. You'd be amazed at how excited people can get when you offer them a free CD, even if it's one or two years old.

Chapter 14

If You Choose
To Continue

Phase Three: Bordering States

As I said earlier, if things are going well after about ten to twelve weeks of the Phase Two promotion, it's time to continue on to Phase Three. In this phase of the release, you will be promoting your record to all the cities within one state of your home state that represent "major markets" for your style of music. (Again, any city with a population over 100,000 that contains at least one good-sized commercial radio station in your format can safely be considered a "major market".) Obviously, any city that was included in Phase Two of the promotion will not be part of the Phase Three expansion, although you should always continue to pursue exposure and sales in any market where you're still getting solid airplay.

Note that during Phase Three you'll be expanding the promotion *only* to cities in states that border your own (unless perhaps you live in a small northeastern state). *This is not the time to expand the promotion to your entire region!* For example, if you're based in Columbus, Ohio, you should be looking at Charleston (WV), Indianapolis (IN), Detroit (MI), and Pittsburgh (PA). This is not the time to try to cover the entire Midwest.

Again, the idea is to keep the campaign manageable for as long as possible so you can devote a sufficient amount of attention to every market, even with limited resources.

The steps you'll need to take to prepare for Phase Three are virtually identical to those in Phase Two. First, identify the cities you'll need to target. Then, get a list of all the significant college, community, and commercial radio stations in those cities. Next, call these stations and find out which stores you'll need to get into. Finally, call the distributor and tell them exactly what you're planning to do and ask them for additional advice regarding which stations and stores you should target.

If you haven't been able to get a distributor up to this point, this would be an excellent time to send out some more packages and try again. If things went well enough in Phase Two to warrant a Phase Three promotion, your story should be compelling enough to at least get you a foot in the door with a quality distributor.

The same goes for booking agents. If you haven't been able to get something going with a regional agency yet, this is an excellent time to try again. But even if you aren't able to get hooked up with a booking agent, there's certainly no reason you can't continue to do the job yourself. You can find a list of the major "talent buyers" in *YPR*. And you can find out the names of the cool, smaller clubs by asking the folks at radio stations and record stores in the area. Because the cities in Phase Three of the promotion will be farther from your home, you'll probably want to arrange little mini-tours in which you visit several cities in one swing—playing gigs, meeting with music directors, doing on-air interviews, in-store performances, etc.

Other than the increased size of the promotion area, Phase Three of the promotion is basically the same as Phase Two: you're going to use your (constantly updated) story to generate excitement about your record as you introduce it into new markets, supported by radio airplay, press coverage, and live performances.

Stroking The Hand That Feeds

As you start to establish a foothold for your record in the Phase Three markets, it's a great idea to go back and thank some of the people in your home city and the Phase Two cities for helping along with way. It doesn't take a lot of effort to send a fax to the music director and DJs of a local station that supported your record early on. In the fax, be sure to describe how their support of your record helped you. Be specific! (Even if you have to stretch the truth a bit.)

For example, you might tell a local music director that his support of the record prompted a commercial station in the next town over to add the record. (There is absolutely *nothing* a college music director likes more than to hear that he "got on" a record before his competitors at commercial radio.) Or you might tell a local DJ that the on-air interview she did helped you get a big gig at a local club or a review in a local paper. And if you have to stretch the truth just a little bit, who does it hurt? The DJ will be thrilled, and you'll have made a friend for life.

Phase Four: Going Regional

After about eight to ten weeks in Phase Three, it's once again time to assess your progress and consider expanding to Phase Four. Once again, you're looking for significant airplay on at least 50% of the stations in the promotion, reviews in local papers, good draws at your live shows, and sales of at least twenty-five records per city per week. If things are going well and you have the resources, continue the promotion into the states bordering the Phase Three states, or at least the ones bordering those states where you're doing well. If, however, less than 50% of the stations are really playing your record and sales and concert attendance are low, it's probably time to end the promotion and think about recalling the record (or at least refocusing your efforts on the current markets before expanding).

Phase Four of the promotion is merely a continuation of Phase Three: pick the cities, stations, stores, and music publications you want to target, work with the distributor to get the record into the area, and then promote it for all you're worth. After about ten weeks, reassess your progress and determine whether you have the "story" and the resources necessary to expand the promotion to other regions.

Phase Five: Going National

If this is your first release, I recommend you limit your promotion to the regional level. For one thing, unless you're getting airplay on dozens of commercial stations and drawing at least 300 people every time you play live, you're going to have a very difficult time getting your record into stores outside your region. For another, conducting a nationwide promotion takes a lot of money, and unless you've got tens of thousands of dollars at your disposal, your resources are probably best spent making and promoting your next record.

On the other hand, if this is your second or third record and you've established a solid base within your region, you might want to consider expanding to the single region closest to you. (If you're in the South, consider expanding to the Midwest. If you're in the Midwest, consider expanding to the South or East, etc.) Again, there is no compelling reason to promote to multiple regions at once, and there are several compelling reasons not to.

If, however, you're an up-and-going independent label and you have the money and the people power to conduct a full-scale national promotion, remember that at this level you'll need to include the national music trade publications in the publicity mail-out. This includes *Gavin, CMJ, FMQB, Album Network*, and *Hard Report*. When sending to these publications, you'll need to send it to the music editor for your format. (As usual, you should call ahead to get the name of the appropriate person.) Getting a review in one or more of these publications can help you get adds at college and commercial radio. If you've never dealt with these publications before, it might be useful to take out a small advertisement as a way of "introducing yourself".

In conducting a national record campaign as an independent artist or label, it's important to have realistic expectations. Unless something truly amazing happens, you're probably not going to be able to get your record stocked nationally by major retail chains (unless you happen to have tens of thousands of dollars to spend on advertising), nor are you going to be able to get significant airplay on major commercial radio stations outside your region. But with good planning and work, you should be able to build upon your earlier success to get your record stocked in indie record stores, played on major college stations, and reviewed in major publications across the country. And that's going to do a great deal to move your career forward, whether you decide to sign with a larger label or remain an independent.

When The Release Is Over, Give Thanks

There's no reason why you can't promote an individual record for as long as six or even nine months. But at some point you're going to have to call it quits. As we discussed earlier, when you decide to end the promotion, the first thing you should do is notify your distributor and then formally recall the record from stores unless you plan to release another record within the next six months. (For instructions on how to recall your record, see above.)

Another thing you should do when the promotion is complete is send out "Thank You" cards to all the people who played a significant role in the success of the release (as well as other important people who only helped a little this time, but whom you hope will help more next time).

If possible, these Thank You cards should be hand-addressed and signed, and should read something like:

Dear _____

Now that the official promotion for <name of record> by <name of group> is finally drawing to a close, we at <name of record label> just want to say thank you for your support during the campaign. With your help, <name of record> was added at over <x> commercial and college radio stations, sold over <x> copies and generated a great deal of exposure for <name of group>. Thanks again. We couldn't have done it without you!

Sincerely,

<your signature>

P.S.—We're looking forward to working with you on our next record, due out in <month of next release>!

Send these cards to music directors at all the college stations that gave your record significant airplay, as well as any commercial music directors that played your record at all. Also, send cards to any writers or editors who gave you a positive review or some other exposure. You might also want to contact your distributor and ask them for the names of the folks at retail who supported your release.

It's Not Dead Yet

And remember, just because you've ended the official promotion does not mean that your record is "dead". As I mentioned earlier, you're going to want to re-release the first record when you come out with your second. Also, keep in mind that for anyone who is just coming in contact with your music for the first time, your record might as well be brand new, no matter how many months ago it was actually "released". There's no reason you can't continue to sell your record and even tour for months after you end the official promotion. And if you *really* start to generate a buzz playing live (and maybe doing some guest appearances on the radio), you might even want to re-release the record in the area where you're having success.

Chapter 15

Measuring Your Success

Unfortunately, there's a tendency among artists new to the record business to think that unless their first record sells hundreds of thousands (or even millions) of copies and propels them to instant fame, their release has been a failure and their careers are in jeapordy. Fortunately, nothing could be further from the truth.

There's an old saying in the music business that goes: "Every overnight success is seven years in the making." And this is what you need to remember in assessing the success of your first release. Even if you don't make a profit on your first record, you'll probably have a lot to feel good about. For one thing, you'll have learned an awful lot about the record business and how it works. For another, you'll have introduced your music to a much wider audience than had heard it previously. And hopefully, you'll have begun to develop a solid fanbase and identified at least a few markets that are very receptive to your music. Finally, you will have established relationships with distributors, retailers, music directors and DJs, music writers, booking agents, talent buyers, other musicians, and maybe even some record people.

In short, by the end of your first release, you'll have begun to develop the skills and establish the relationships that will be critical to your long-term success in this business.

Your Next Release(s)

Assuming you don't get signed off your first release (most bands don't), now is the time to start thinking about making your next record. You should try to come out with your second record within twelve months of your first release. If you can't manage that, you should definitely try to come out with *something* no more than eighteen months after your first release. Any longer than that and the base you worked so hard to establish during the first release will begin to erode.

Basically, the second release is going to be just the like the first one, only bigger and better. Because this time, you're going to have a much larger number of personal contacts on which to draw. Not only will you have developed personal relationships with various music directors, DJs, writers, and retailers, but you will also have started to develop your fan base and mailing list. In addition, you will have identified markets in your area that are receptive to your music, and in general, you'll have a much better idea about how to run a record release.

Because you've already established this foundation, I recommend that you include in Phase One of your second release not only your home base city, but also those cities in Phase Two of your initial release that showed a positive response to your music. In other words, the second time around, you should be able to make a bigger splash initially by including several "friendly" cities in your Phase One promotion. This will help you extend the reach of your second release farther (and more productively) than your first.

Other than that, just remember to apply all the same techniques you used with success during the first release: send packages via Priority Mail; include memorable trinkets; follow up religiously; use each success to create others; and if you're trying to get signed to a larger label, keep them updated as to your progress.

Chapter 16

Getting Signed

Over the course of this book, I've tried to make clear the benefits of releasing your own records and maintaining control over the course of your career. But for those of you who are still convinced that a major label (or a large independent) is where you need to be, here are some suggestions as to how you might best bring yourself to the attention of those who hold the purse strings.

First, do not—repeat *do not!*— send mass mailings of your demo tape, or even your CD, to major label A&R reps. At best, this will prove to be nothing more than a waste of your time and money. Even if an A&R rep loves your material, the odds that he'll offer you a deal worth signing are close to zero.

Instead, before you release your record, make a list of ten successful artists in your format whose work you admire, and find out what labels they're on. If you've made contacts at booking agencies, management companies, and/or record labels, ask them to suggest the labels that are best suited to you and your music.

Once you've made a list of the ten or so labels you're going to target, go to the *Sourcebook* and find out the names of the people at these labels who have the authority to sign new bands. Contrary to what most people think, most A&R reps do *not* have the authority to sign new bands. This authority is usually limited to the people listed as "vice president" or "senior director" of A&R.

If your copy of the *Sourcebook* is more than one year old, you should call the label to make sure the VP in question still works there. (Turnover at record labels is incredibly high, especially among executives.)

Then, just as you begin Phase Two of the release, send each person on your "A&R list" a package containing your record and a very brief letter in which you explain your plans for the current release and request that they listen to your record. If you've succeeded in targeting the people at the label who actually have the authority to sign you, you're going to have a very difficult time getting them to listen to your record. Don't be discouraged, and don't give up (unless they explicitly ask you to stop contacting them). Instead, send brief fax updates every two weeks to the people on your list to make them aware of the progress of your release. (Once again, these regular updates are only effective if you're actually making progress. If you're not, stop faxing and get back out there and make something happen!)

Eventually, you should be able to get some of these people to listen to your material. When you do, ask them how they liked it. Recap for them the progress you've made so far, and briefly describe what you have planned for the future. Your attitude should be: "I'd love to be on your label, but even if you don't sign me, I'm going to find a way to be successful, because I know what I need to do, and I know how to do it." There's no need to hype yourself, and there's no need to lie. If you're going to get signed, it's going to be because you got your material to the right person at the right time and convinced them that you would succeed on their label by first succeeding on your own.

In other words, if it's gonna happen, it's gonna happen. So don't stress. Just go out there and promote your record and let the rest take care of itself. To do anything else is just a waste of time.

Still Have Questions?

My goal in writing this book was to help you learn what you need to know in order to take control of your own destiny and make a career of recording and performing original music. I've done my best to include every tip I could think of to help you make your release a success.

Now it's up to you. So go out there and give it your best shot. And when you do, drop me a line to let me know how it's going. If you have specific questions about your release or your music career, fill out the "Free Consulting Services" form in the back of this book, and send it to me along with a copy of your CD (and any other material you care to include). I'll do my best to send you a reply within three weeks of receiving your package. (For fastest reply, be sure to include your email address.)

Thanks, and good luck!

Tim Sweeney

Appendix A:

21 Things You Should Do To Make Your Release A Success

1. Finish writing and arranging your songs *before* you enter the studio.
2. Have your record mixed and mastered by a proven professional.
3. Make CDs. (Don't make cassettes.)
4. Register with the Uniform Code Council and get a bar code for your CD.
5. Don't include a band photo anywhere on your album art, unless it's a really good photograph.
6. Make your one-sheet compelling.
7. Spend the time necessary to find and develop a relationship with a quality distributor.
8. Make your press kit memorable and brief.
9. Selecting a home base city that makes sense for your release.
10. If you don't live in or near a market that's appropriate for your music—move.
11. Select the radio stations in your promotion carefully. Send only to the stations that can really do you some good.
12. Keep your initial release small, then expand slowly.
13. Follow up. Follow up. Follow up.
14. Wield the power of the fax to your best advantage.
15. Get good gigs, and promote them as if your entire career depends on it. (It does.)
16. When you finish playing, come down off the front of the stage and introduce yourself to every single person in the crowd, every single time.

17. Don't count on using money from initial sales to fund the later stages of your campaign. (You're not going to get most of that money until after the release is over.)
18. Assess your progress after each phase of your release.
19. Recall your record when retailers start returning it to the distributor.
20. Don't try to substitute money for hard work.
21. Don't ask others to do for you what you can do better for yourself.

Appendix B

Some Names & Numbers To Get You Started

College Music Journal (CMJ)
(516) 466-6000

Gavin Report
(415) 495-1990

Pollstar
(209) 224-2631

The Recording Industry Sourcebook
c/o Mix Bookshelf
(800) 233-9604

The Uniform Code Council (the bar code people)
(513) 435-3870

Yahoo (worldwide web directory)
http://www.yahoo.com/

Yellow Pages of Rock (YPR)
(818) 955-4000

Order Form

Tim Sweeney's Guide To Releasing Independent Records

❑ *$27.95* (non-CA residents)
❑ *$30.00* (CA residents only)

Both prices includes $3 shipping.

NAME _____

ADDRESS _____

_____

PHONE ( ) _____

FAX ( ) _____

EMAIL _____

❑ Check ❑ Visa ❑ MasterCard

Credit card no. _____

Exp. Date _____

To order: call (310) 542-6430
fax (310) 542-1300

Send check to: TSA BOOKS
21213-B Hawthorne Blvd. #5255
Torrance, CA 90503.

Free Consulting Services!

If you have specific questions you'd like to ask Tim Sweeney about your independent release or your music career, fill out this form and mail it along with a copy of your CD and your promo package to the address below. Allow three weeks for a response. (Only packages containing this form will receive a reply.)

Please Type Or Print Clearly

your name _____

name of band _____

name of record _____

name of label _____

address _____

_____

phone (   ) _____   fax (   ) _____

email address _____

question(s): _____

_____

_____

_____

_____

_____

Mail to: **Free Consulting Services**
          TSA
          21213-B Hawthorne Blvd. #5255
          Torrance, CA 90503